# Collins

# The Shangh Maths Project

**For the English National Curriculum**

# Homework Guide 3

Author: Paul Broadbent

Homework Guide Series Editor: Amanda Simpson

Practice Books Series Editor: Professor Lianghuo Fan

# Contents

**Chapter 1 Revising and improving**
1.1 Revision for addition and subtraction of 2-digit numbers ... 4
1.2 Addition and subtraction (1) ... 5
1.3 Addition and subtraction (2) ... 6
1.4 Calculating smartly ... 7
1.5 What number should be in the box? ... 8
1.6 Let's revise multiplication ... 9
1.7 Games of multiplication and division ... 10

**Chapter 2 Multiplication and division (II)**
2.1 Multiplying and dividing by 7 ... 11
2.2 Multiplying and dividing by 3 ... 12
2.3 Multiplying and dividing by 6 ... 13
2.4 Multiplying and dividing by 9 ... 14
2.5 Relationships between multiplications of 3, 6 and 9 ... 15
2.6 Multiplication grid ... 16
2.7 Posing multiplication and division questions (1) ... 17
2.8 Posing multiplication and division questions (2) ... 19
2.9 Using multiplication and addition to express a number ... 20
2.10 Division with a remainder ... 21
2.11 Calculation of division with a remainder (1) ... 22
2.12 Calculation of division with a remainder (2) ... 23
2.13 Calculation of division with a remainder (3) ... 24

**Chapter 3 Knowing numbers up to 1000**
3.1 Knowing numbers up to 1000 (1) ... 25
3.2 Knowing numbers up to 1000 (2) ... 27
3.3 Number lines (to 1000) (1) ... 28
3.4 Number lines (to 1000) (2) ... 29
3.5 Fun with the place value chart (1) ... 30
3.6 Fun with the place value chart (2) ... 31

**Chapter 4 Statistics (II)**
4.1 From statistical tables to bar charts ... 32
4.2 Bar charts (1) ... 33
4.3 Bar charts (2) ... 34

**Chapter 5 Introduction to time (III)**
5.1 Second and minute ... 35
5.2 Times on 12-hour and 24-hour clocks and in Roman numerals ... 36
5.3 Leap years and common years ... 37
5.4 Calculating the duration of time ... 38

**Chapter 6 Consolidation and enhancement**
6.1 5 threes plus 3 threes equals 8 threes ... 39
6.2 5 threes minus 3 threes equals 2 threes ... 40
6.3 Multiplication and division ... 41
6.4 Mathematics plaza – dots and patterns ... 42
6.5 Mathematics plaza – magic square ... 43
6.6 Numbers to 1000 and beyond ... 44
6.7 Read, write and compare numbers to 1000 and beyond ... 45

**Chapter 7 Addition and subtraction with 3-digit numbers**
7.1 Addition and subtraction of whole hundreds and tens (1) ... 46
7.2 Addition and subtraction of whole hundreds and tens (2) ... 47
7.3 Adding and subtracting 3-digit numbers and ones (1) ... 48

7.4  Adding and subtracting 3-digit
     numbers and ones (2)                49
7.5  Addition with 3-digit numbers (1)   50
7.6  Addition with 3-digit numbers (2)   51
7.7  Subtraction with 3-digit
     numbers (1)                         52
7.8  Subtraction with 3-digit
     numbers (2)                         53
7.9  Estimating addition and subtraction
     with 3-digit numbers (1)            54
7.10 Estimating addition and subtraction
     with 3-digit numbers (2)            55

## Chapter 8 Simple fractions and their addition and subtraction

8.1  Unit fractions and tenths           56
8.2  Non-unit fractions                  57
8.3  Equivalent fractions                58
8.4  Addition and subtraction of
     simple fractions                    59

## Chapter 9 Multiplying and dividing by a 1-digit number

9.1  Multiplying by whole tens
     and hundreds (1)                    60
9.2  Multiplying by whole tens
     and hundreds (2)                    61
9.3  Writing number sentences            62
9.4  Multiplying a 2-digit number
     by a 1-digit number (1)             63
9.5  Multiplying a 2-digit number
     by a 1-digit number (2)             64
9.6  Multiplying a 2-digit number
     by a 1-digit number (3)             65
9.7  Multiplying a 3-digit number
     by a 1-digit number (1)             66
9.8  Multiplying a 3-digit number
     by a 1-digit number (2)             67
9.9  Practice and exercise               68
9.10 Dividing whole tens and
     whole hundreds                      69
9.11 Dividing a 2-digit number
     by a 1-digit number (1)             70
9.12 Dividing a 2-digit number
     by a 1-digit number (2)             71
9.13 Dividing a 2-digit number
     by a 1-digit number (3)             72
9.14 Dividing a 2-digit number
     by a 1-digit number (4)             73
9.15 Dividing a 2-digit number
     by a 1-digit number (5)             74
9.16 Dividing a 3-digit number
     by a 1-digit number (1)             75
9.17 Dividing a 3-digit number
     by a 1-digit number (2)             76
9.18 Dividing a 3-digit number
     by a 1-digit number (3)             77
9.19 Application of division             78
9.20 Finding the total price             79

## Chapter 10 Let's practise geometry

10.1 Angles                              80
10.2 Identifying different types
     of line (1)                         81
10.3 Identifying different types
     of line (2)                         82
10.4 Drawing 2-D shapes and
     making 3-D shapes                   83
10.5 Length: metre, centimetre
     and millimetre                      84
10.6 Perimeters of simple
     2-D shapes (1)                      85
10.7 Perimeters of simple
     2-D shapes (2)                      86

**Answers**                              87

# 1.1 Revision for addition and subtraction of 2-digit numbers

## Add and subtract 2-digit numbers

1. Look at these.

    34 + 65 = 99             33 + 66 = 99

    Make up six more additions that have a sum of 99.

    _____             _____

    _____             _____

    _____             _____

2. Add up the columns and rows in the grey boxes and write the totals in the white boxes. Work out the missing numbers for (c) and (d).

    (a) 
    | 23 | 31 |   |
    |----|----|---|
    | 28 | 45 |   |
    |    |    |   |

    (b)
    | 32 | 29 |   |
    |----|----|---|
    | 38 | 37 |   |
    |    |    |   |

    (c)
    |    | 31 |    |
    |----|----|----|
    | 22 |    | 57 |
    | 46 |    |    |

    (d)
    | 46 |    |    |
    |----|----|----|
    |    | 39 | 68 |
    |    | 75 |    |

3. This chart shows the number of balls made in a factory over three days. Write the totals.

    | | Footballs | Basketballs | Netballs | Total number of balls each day |
    |---|---|---|---|---|
    | Day 1 | 22 | 36 | 41 | |
    | Day 2 | 34 | 32 | 33 | |
    | Day 3 | 28 | 27 | 25 | |
    | Total of each ball | | | | |

## Addition squares

Draw addition squares like those in Question 2 for your child to try to complete. Put four numbers in any of the boxes and ask your child to work out the missing numbers. Check that they use the numbers they are given to help them and ask if they are using addition or subtraction to work out each missing number.

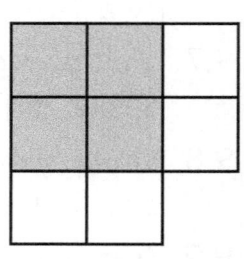

4                                                                       ©HarperCollinsPublishers 2018

# 1.2 Addition and subtraction (1)

## Add and subtract 2-digit numbers

1. Write the number sentences and calculate.

   (a) 27 girls 18 boys

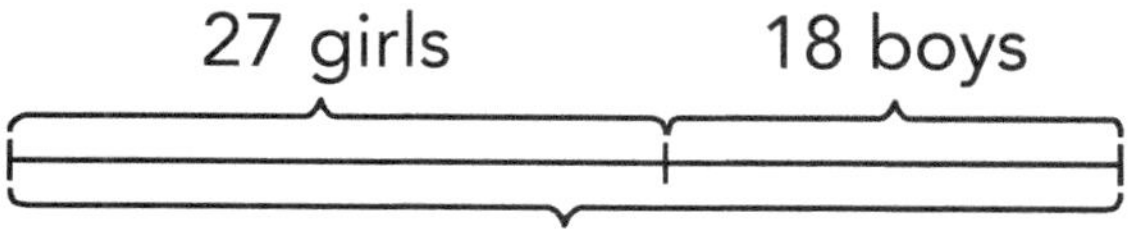

   How many children are there in total?

   Number sentence: _____

   Answer: ☐

   (b) 34 roses ? tulips

   66 flowers in total

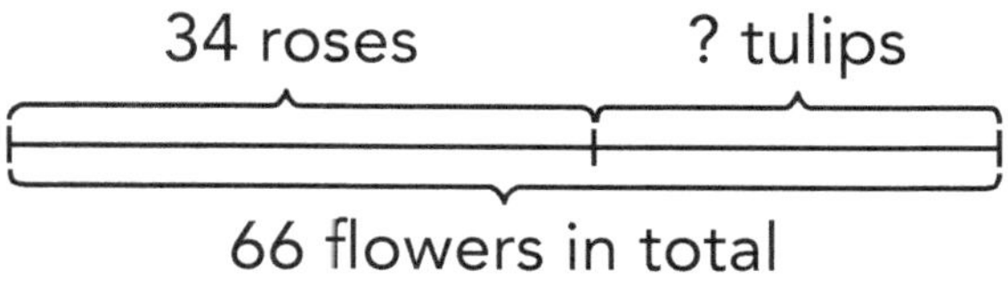

   How many tulips are there?

   Number sentence: _____

   Answer: ☐

   (c) 39 red cars

   5 more blue cars than red cars

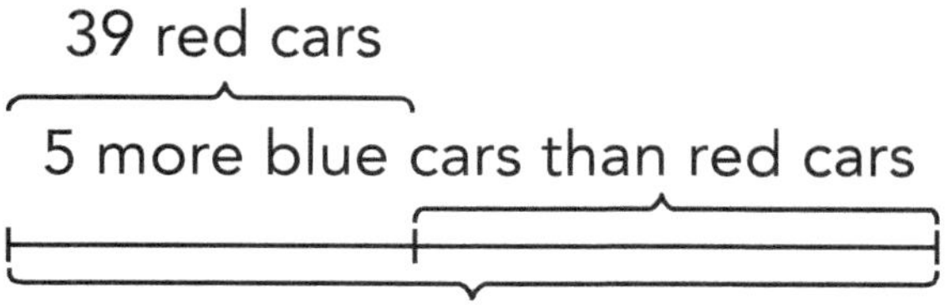

   How many cars are there?

   Number sentence: _____

   Answer: ☐

   (d) 42 oranges

   26 pineapples

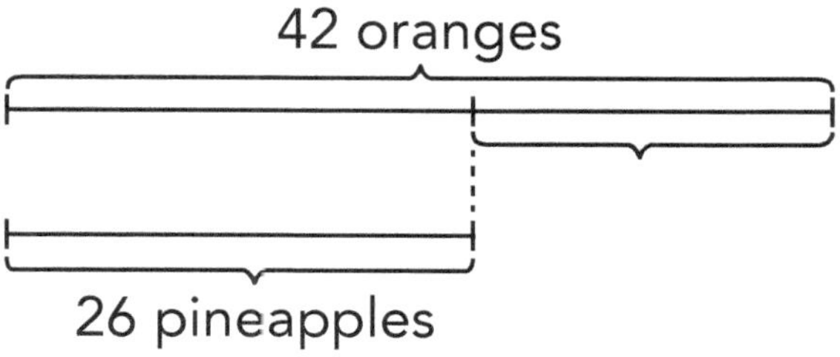

   How many more oranges are there than pineapples?

   Number sentence: _____

   Answer: ☐

2. Write each number sentence and calculate.

   (a) There were 85 apples for Year 3 children on Monday. After morning break there were 23 apples left. How many apples had been eaten by the children in Year 3 on Monday?

   Number sentence: _____

   (b) In a car park there were 46 vehicles. 29 were cars and the rest were vans. How many vans were in the car park?

   Number sentence: _____

   (c) Jan and Sam both rolled a 1p coin. Jan rolled hers 52 cm, which was 17 cm further than Sam rolled his. How far did Sam roll his coin?

   Number sentence: _____

### 👥 Bar line model

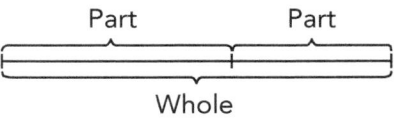

Part Part

Whole

Question 1 uses bar line models to help your child make sense of the problems. They show a whole number broken into parts which can then have numbers inserted to show the calculation that is needed. Talk about the bar line model with your child to check their understanding.

©HarperCollinsPublishers 2018

# 1.3 Addition and subtraction (2)

## Add and subtract 2-digit numbers

1. Write the number sentences and calculate.

   (a)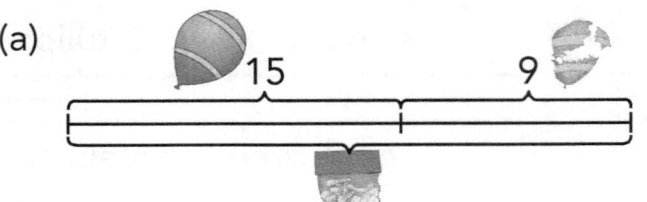

   How many balloons were in the packet?

   Number sentence: _____

   (b)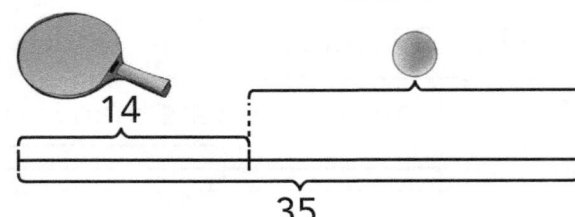

   How many eggs are not broken?

   Number sentence: _____

   (c)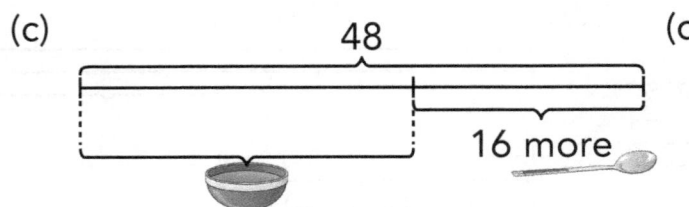

   How many bowls are there?

   Number sentence: _____

   (d) 

   How many fewer bats than balls?

   Number sentence: _____

2. Answer these.

     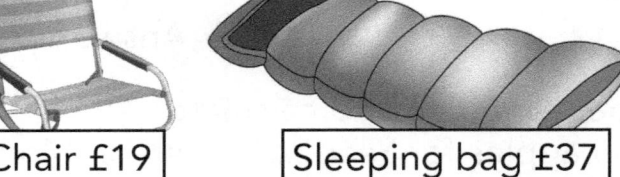 

   Tent £63    Chair £19    Sleeping bag £37    BBQ £47

   (a) The Bun family bought two camping items for exactly £100. Which items did they buy?

   Number sentence: _____

   (b) Mr Hart bought a chair and a tent. How much did he spend?

   Number sentence: _____

   (c) Mrs Tay had £50 and bought a sleeping bag. How much has she left?

   Number sentence: _____

##  Using bar line models

For Question 2, ask your child if they can draw a bar line model to show each example. They will still have to add or subtract using a mental or written method, but the bar line model will show if they have understood the problem correctly.

# 1.4 Calculating smartly

## Use strategies to add and subtract 2-digit numbers

**1.** Write the missing numbers.

(a) 37 + 18 = ☐
↓
36 + 19  ↑
↓
35 + 20 = ☐

(b) 43 + 36 = ☐
↓
42 + 37  ↑
↓
41 + 38
↓
40 + 39 = ☐

(c) 53 − 24 = ☐
↓
52 − 23  ↑
↓
51 − 22
↓
50 − 21
↓
49 − 20 = ☐

(d) 75 − 48 = ☐
↓
76 − 49  ↑
↓
77 − 50 = ☐

**2.** Complete these.

(a) 58 + 27 = ☐
   + 2  − 2   ↑
   ↓   ↓
   60 + 25 = ☐

(b) 65 − 47 = ☐
   + 3  + 3   ↑
   ↓   ↓
   68 − 50 = ☐

(c) 39 + 43 = ☐
   ☐  ☐
   ↓  ↓   ↑
   ☐ + ☐ = ☐

(d) 57 − 18 = ☐
   ☐  ☐
   ↓  ↓   ↑
   ☐ − ☐ = ☐

**3.** Calculate smartly.

(a) 59 + 13 = 60 + ☐ = ☐

(b) 65 − 38 = ☐ − 40 = ☐

(c) 27 + 24 = ☐ + ☐ = ☐

(d) 86 − 47 = ☐ − ☐ = ☐

## 👨‍👦 Keeping it balanced

**You will need:** balance scales, 20 sweets (in two colours).

Being smart about calculating in the questions on this sheet involves adding and subtracting numbers to make the calculation easier to work with, while keeping the answer the same.

Using a simpler example, 4 + 9 gives the same answer as 3 + 10 (subtract 1 from 4 and add 1 to 9), which is easier to calculate. Balance scales can be used to model this, with sweets that are two colours but otherwise the same swapped over to show that the answer stays the same – the scales stay balanced.

©HarperCollinsPublishers 2018

# 1.5 What number should be in the box?

## Solve missing number addition and subtraction problems

1. Look at the diagrams and fill in the boxes.

   (a)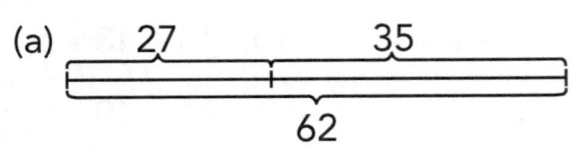

   (b)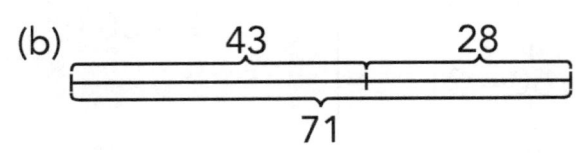

   ☐ + ☐ = ☐      ☐ + ☐ = ☐
   ☐ − ☐ = ☐      ☐ − ☐ = ☐
   ☐ + ☐ = ☐      ☐ + ☐ = ☐
   ☐ − ☐ = ☐      ☐ − ☐ = ☐

2. Complete these.

   (a)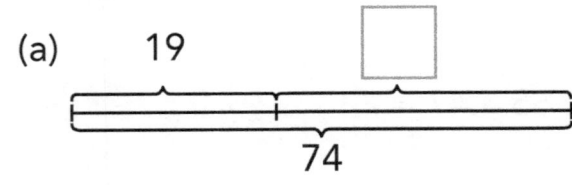

   (b)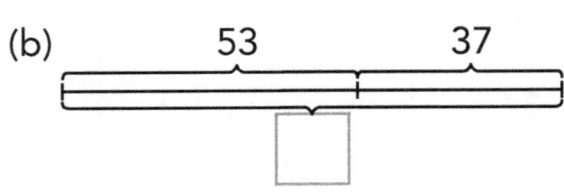

   (c)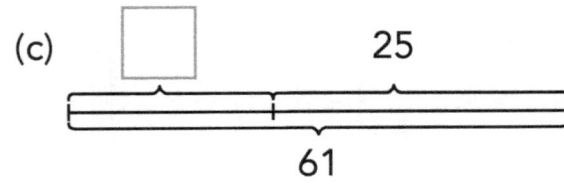

   19 + ☐ = 74
   74 − 19 = ☐
   ☐ − 53 = 37
   53 + 37 = ☐
   ☐ + 25 = 61     61 − ☐ = 25
   61 − 25 = ☐     61 − 25 = ☐

3. The digits 1 to 8 are missing. Complete the calculations by writing the digits in the correct box.

   | 1 | 2 | 3 | 4 |
   | 5 | 6 | 7 | 8 |

   (a) ☐☐ + 34 = 62      (b) 47 + ☐☐ = 63

   (c) ☐☐ − 28 = 45      (d) 86 − ☐☐ = 32

## 👪 Finding pairs

**You will need:** a 100 square, counters in two colours.

Make a 100 square on a 10 × 10 grid by writing each of the numbers 1–100 in the spaces, in order, starting from the top left corner and completing the rows from left to right, so number 1 is top left and 100 is bottom right. Alternatively, you can use a snakes and ladders board.

Give yourself and your child different coloured counters and take turns to cover pairs of numbers that total 50. Write the calculations down and then put them in this order so your child can see the patterns between the numbers and on the square: 25 + 25, 24 + 26, 23 + 27, … Change the tasks to find pairs that total 99 or a number your child chooses. You can also find pairs of numbers with a difference of 30 or 25.

# 1.6 Let's revise multiplication

## Use the relationship between the 2, 4 and 8 times tables

1. Fill in the missing numbers.

| × | 1 | 2 | 3 | 4 | 5 | 6 | 7 | 8 | 9 | 10 | 11 | 12 |
|---|---|---|---|---|---|---|---|---|---|----|----|----|
| 2 | 2 | 4 | 6 |   |   | 12 | 14 |   |   |   |   |   |
| 4 | 4 | 8 |   | 16 |   |   |   |   | 36 |   |   | 48 |
| 8 | 8 | 16 |   |   | 40 |   |   | 64 |   | 80 |   |   |

2. Use doubles to help answer these.

(a) 6 × 2 = ☐    (b) 7 × 4 = ☐    (c) 4 × 3 = ☐

   6 × 4 = ☐       7 × 8 = ☐       8 × 3 = ☐

(d) 4 × 12 = ☐   (e) 8 × 4 = ☐    (f) 2 × 11 = ☐

   8 × 12 = ☐      8 × 8 = ☐       4 × 11 = ☐

3. Use the digits 0 to 5.

   [0] [1] [2] [3] [4] [5]

   Find a place for each of the digits:

   (a) ☐ × ☐ = 12    (b) ☐ × 5 = ☐0    (c) ☐ × 8 = 4☐

---

### 👪 Three in a row

Play the game 'Three in a row' with your child. Copy the grid from Question 1 with all the boxes filled in. Shuffle and lay the number cards face down in a pile. If you have a blank dice, label two sides with each of × 2, × 4 and × 8. For a 1–6 dice use the following:

1 and 2 = × 2

3 and 4 = × 4

5 and 6 = × 8

**You will need:** counters, dice, number cards 1–12.

Take turns to play. Turn over the top card and then roll the dice. Calculate the answer and then place a counter over the matching square in the grid. Keep playing until a player wins by getting three counters in a row horizontally or vertically.

# 1.7 Games of multiplication and division

## Use multiplication and division facts to solve problems

When the shopping was delivered, there were some packs of eggs:

1. Write the number sentences and calculate.
   (a) How many days will the eggs last if 6 are eaten each day?

   (b) How many days will the eggs last if 2 are eaten each day?

   (c) How many days will the eggs last if 3 are eaten each day?

   (d) How many days will the eggs last if 4 are eaten each day?


2. How many tomatoes are there in total? Group them in two different ways and write the number sentences.

(a) ☐ × ☐ + ☐ = ☐            (b) ☐ × ☐ + ☐ = ☐

☐ × ☐ − ☐ = ☐            ☐ × ☐ − ☐ = ☐

## 👪 Grouping pegs

Give your child a pile of about 20 clothes pegs and ask them to group them in different ways, for example in groups of 2, 3 or 4. Can they find ways of grouping them so that there are no pegs left over, then 1 left over, 2 left over, 3 left over and so on?

**You will need:** 20 clothes pegs.

Ask them to record their solutions as number sentences:

5 groups of 4 with 1 left over is 21 pegs      $5 × 4 + 1 = 21$

# 2.1 Multiplying and dividing by 7

## Multiply and divide by 7

1. Complete these.
   (a) 2 × 7 = ☐
   (b) ☐ × 7 = 70
   (c) 8 × ☐ = 56
   (d) ☐ × 7 = 21
   (e) 6 × 7 = ☐
   (f) 7 × ☐ = 77
   (g) 7 ÷ ☐ = 1
   (h) 49 ÷ 7 = ☐
   (i) 63 ÷ ☐ = 9
   (j) ☐ ÷ 4 = 7
   (k) 35 ÷ ☐ = 5
   (l) 84 ÷ 7 = ☐

2. Look at these number machines and complete each chart.

   (a)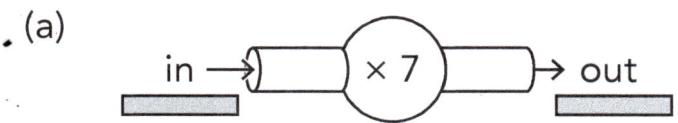

   | In | 3 | 7 | 4 | 9 | 6 | 12 |
   |---|---|---|---|---|---|---|
   | Out | | | | | | |

   (b)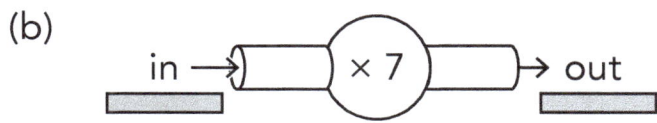

   | In | | | | | | |
   |---|---|---|---|---|---|---|
   | Out | 14 | 35 | 56 | 70 | 77 | 7 |

3. Answer these.
   (a) The Grey family go on holiday for 14 days. How many weeks are they on holiday?
   (b) There are 7 tubes of tennis balls and each tube has 3 balls. How many tennis balls are there altogether?
   (c) An egg box holds 6 eggs. 42 eggs are put into egg boxes. How many full boxes of eggs will there be?
   (d) At a sports day there will be 7 basketball teams with 5 players and 4 netball teams with 7 players. Every player will be given a drink. How many drinks are needed altogether?
   (e) The drinks cups are sold in packs of 7. How many packs of cups will need to be bought?

## Learning the 7 times table

The 7 times table is often the most difficult one for children to learn. Encourage your child to use the other times tables to help learn the 7 times table. For example, 7 × 4 is the same as 4 × 7, so you can use the 4 times table to recall the answer 28.

A strategy that may help is to break the 7 × into 5 × and then 2 × to reach the answer. This is useful if your child knows the 5 and 2 times tables. Here is an example:

7 × 6 = ?   5 × 6 = 30
            2 × 6 = 12
            7 × 6 = 42

©HarperCollinsPublishers 2018

# 2.2 Multiplying and dividing by 3

## Multiply and divide by 3

1. Fill in the boxes.

    (a) 8 × 3 = ☐      (b) 3 × 5 = ☐      (c) 3 × 11 = ☐

    (d) 9 × 3 = ☐      (e) 7 × 3 = ☐      (f) 30 ÷ 3 = ☐

    (g) 36 ÷ 3 = ☐     (h) 18 ÷ 3 = ☐

    (i) 27 ÷ 3 = ☐     (j) 6 ÷ 3 = ☐

2. Complete these.

    (a) 6 × 2 = ☐ × 3      (b) 30 ÷ 5 = 3 × ☐      (c) 9 × ☐ = 3 × 6

    (d) ☐ × 3 = 7 + 8      (e) 15 – ☐ = 27 ÷ 3      (f) 3 × 12 = 6 × ☐

3. Fill in the table.

| Dividend | 21 | 30 | 15 |   | 36 |    | 27 |
|----------|----|----|----|---|----|----|----|
| Divisor  |    |    | 5  | 3 |    | 11 | 3  |
| Quotient | 3  | 10 |    | 8 | 12 | 3  |    |

4. A shop has some bikes and some trikes.
   The bikes have 2 wheels and the trikes have 3 wheels.
   Ben counted 4 bikes and 23 wheels altogether.
   How many trikes are there?

---

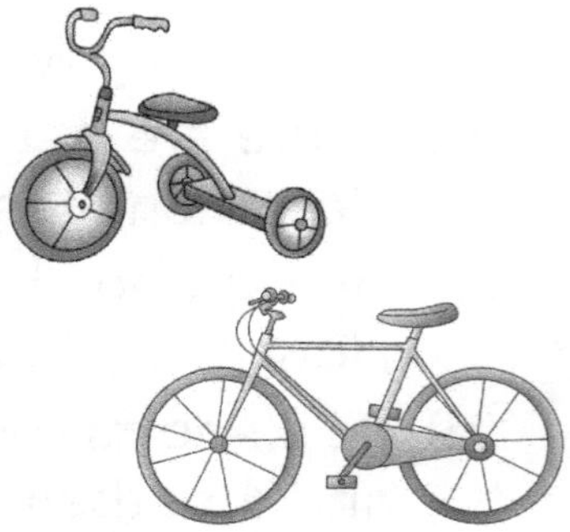

## 👪 Bikes and trikes

The problem for Question 4 is best solved by practically trying out the problem. Give your child some counters or cubes to put in groups of 2 and 3 as if they were the wheels on the bikes and trikes. If they arrange them in two columns they can then look at the combination to make a total of 23 wheels. This table shows that the bikes have 8 wheels so there must be 5 trikes, with 15 wheels to make a total of 23 wheels.

Make up other problems like this, for example, 'If there are 16 wheels altogether and more trikes than bikes, how many trikes are there?'

You will need:
23 counters.

| Bike wheels | Trike wheels |
|-------------|--------------|
| 2           | 3            |
| 4           | 6            |
| 6           | 9            |
| 8           | 12           |
| 10          | 15           |

# 2.3 Multiplying and dividing by 6

## Multiply and divide by 6

1. Follow the instructions to complete this 1–60 number grid.

| 1 | 2 | 3 | 4 | 5 | 6 | 7 | 8 | 9 | 10 |
|---|---|---|---|---|---|---|---|---|---|
| 11 | 12 | 13 | 14 | 15 | 16 | 17 | 18 | 19 | 20 |
| 21 | 22 | 23 | 24 | 25 | 26 | 27 | 28 | 29 | 30 |
| 31 | 32 | 33 | 34 | 35 | 36 | 37 | 38 | 39 | 40 |
| 41 | 42 | 43 | 44 | 45 | 46 | 47 | 48 | 49 | 50 |
| 51 | 52 | 53 | 54 | 55 | 56 | 57 | 58 | 59 | 60 |

Colour all the even numbers yellow.
Circle all the numbers in the 3 times table. Keep going to 60.
Cross through all the numbers in the 6 times table.
What patterns do you notice?

_____

2. Complete these. Colour the facts that you can recall quickly.

   (a) 6 × 1 =          (b) 6 × 5 =          (c) 6 × 9 =
   
   (d) 6 × 2 =          (e) 6 × 6 =          (f) 6 × 10 =
   
   (g) 6 × 3 =          (h) 6 × 7 =          (i) 6 × 11 =
   
   (j) 6 × 4 =          (k) 6 × 8 =          (l) 6 × 12 =

3. Fill in the ◯ with >, < or = .

   (a) 3 × 10 ◯ 6 × 5          (b) 6 × 8 ◯ 46
   
   (c) 6 × 7 ◯ 6 × 6 + 6       (d) 42 ÷ 7 ◯ 24 ÷ 6

## 👪 Egg box maths

Ask your child to take a handful of the counters and to estimate how many they think they have. Then share the counters out into equal groups in the six compartments of the egg box. Any they have left over they pile up next to the box. They then count the counters in one compartment and multiply it by 6. Finally they add on the counters left over and this should give them the total. They compare this with their estimate.

**You will need:**
an egg box that holds six eggs, a pile of counters.

©HarperCollinsPublishers 2018

# 2.4 Multiplying and dividing by 9

## Multiply and divide by 9

1. Continue the patterns.

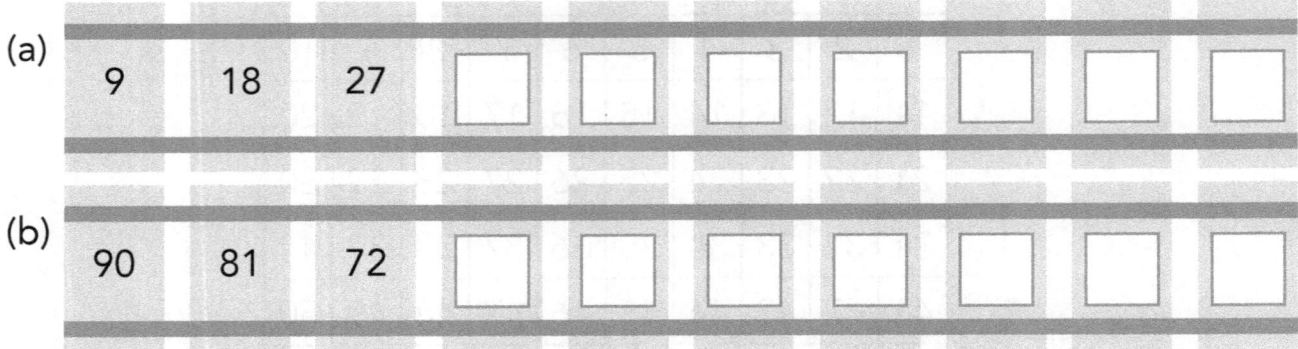

   (a) 9, 18, 27, ☐ ☐ ☐ ☐ ☐ ☐ ☐

   (b) 90, 81, 72, ☐ ☐ ☐ ☐ ☐ ☐ ☐

   What do you notice?

2. Answer these.

   (a) Nine cinema tickets cost £45. What was the cost of each cinema ticket?

   (b) There are 9 boxes of pencils and each box has 4 pencils. How many pencils are there in total?

   (c) 72 chairs were needed for a school assembly and there were 9 chairs in each row. How many rows were there?

   (d) On a school trip, children were put into groups of 9. How many groups of children would fit on a 54-seat bus?

## 👨‍👦 Finger nines

The 9 times table is a lovely set of multiplication facts to learn. A popular way of showing the numbers in the 9 times table is to put both hands with fingers open in front of you. Put any single finger down and note its position. The number of fingers to the left of that bent finger shows the tens value and the number of fingers to the right shows the ones value.

This is the fourth finger and it shows 3 tens (on the left) and 6 ones (on the right). 4 × 9 = 36

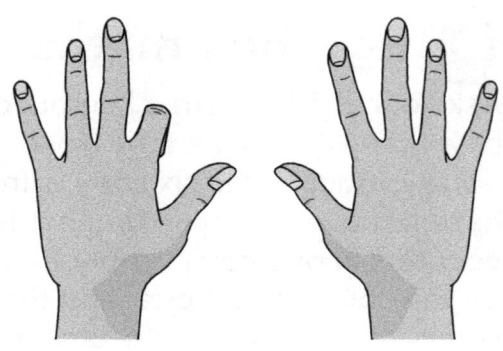

# 2.5 Relationships between multiplications of 3, 6 and 9

## Use the relationship between the 3, 6 and 9 times tables

1. Follow the instructions to complete this 1–60 number grid.

| 1 | 2 | 3 | 4 | 5 | 6 | 7 | 8 | 9 | 10 |
|---|---|---|---|---|---|---|---|---|---|
| 11 | 12 | 13 | 14 | 15 | 16 | 17 | 18 | 19 | 20 |
| 21 | 22 | 23 | 24 | 25 | 26 | 27 | 28 | 29 | 30 |
| 31 | 32 | 33 | 34 | 35 | 36 | 37 | 38 | 39 | 40 |
| 41 | 42 | 43 | 44 | 45 | 46 | 47 | 48 | 49 | 50 |
| 51 | 52 | 53 | 54 | 55 | 56 | 57 | 58 | 59 | 60 |

Colour all the numbers in the 3 times table red.
Circle all the numbers in the 6 times table.
Cross through all the numbers in the 9 times table.
What patterns do you notice?

_____

2. Complete each multiplication so that they equal the star number.

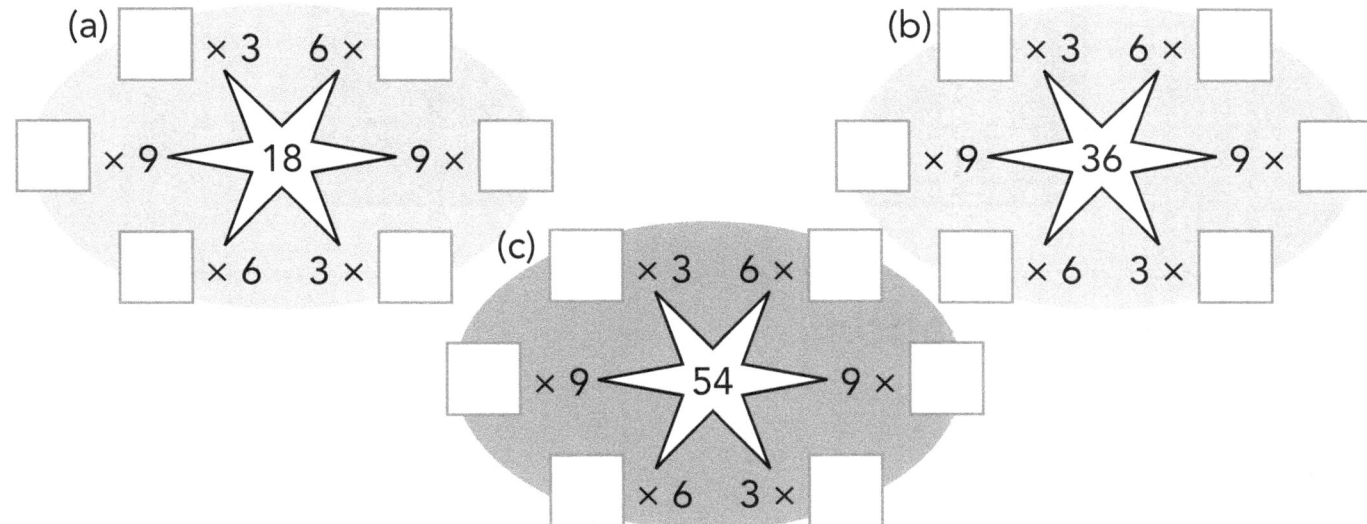

## 👨‍👧 Dividing 36

Ask your child to complete this division fact in six different ways.
Ask them which multiplication facts they used to help them.

36 ÷ ☐ = ☐

To help, they could make different rectangle arrays with 36 counters or buttons.

**You will need:**
36 counters.

©HarperCollinsPublishers 2018

# 2.6 Multiplication grid

## Explore numbers in a multiplication grid

Follow the instructions below to play the dice multiplication game

| 6  | 12 | 36 | 10 | 2  | 24 |
|----|----|----|----|----|----|
| 18 | 25 | 1  | 30 | 18 | 5  |
| 3  | 9  | 8  | 16 | 4  | 20 |
| 30 | 15 | 24 | 15 | 9  | 4  |

| 1  | 30 | 12 | 24 | 4  | 3  |
|----|----|----|----|----|----|
| 20 | 8  | 30 | 4  | 15 | 9  |
| 10 | 6  | 18 | 15 | 9  | 36 |
| 5  | 24 | 25 | 16 | 18 | 2  |

 **Dice multiplication**

Play the multiplying game using the two gameboards above. It is a game for two players.

**To play**

Each player chooses their gameboard.

Take turns to roll two dice (or one dice twice) and multiply the numbers together.

Use a counter to cover a square on your gameboard that matches your answer. If you cannot go, miss that turn and pass the dice over.

The winner is the first player to cover four squares in a vertical line.

**Challenge**

Change the rule to win by being the first player to cover a horizontal line of six squares.

**You will need:** counters for each player, two 1–6 dice (or numbers 1–6 written on small pieces of paper).

# 2.7 Posing multiplication and division questions (1)

## Write multiplication and division number sentences

1. Write four different facts for each number. Group the dots to help you.

(a) ▢ × ▢   ▢ × ▢   12   ▢ × ▢   ▢ × ▢

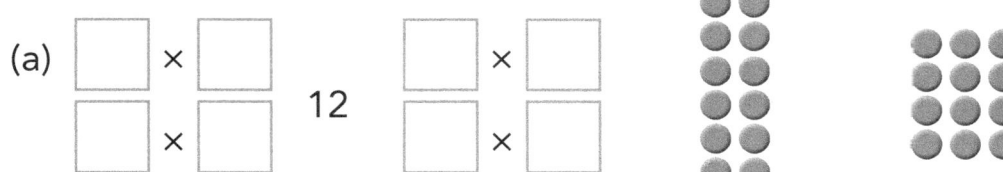

(b) ▢ × ▢   ▢ × ▢   18   ▢ × ▢   ▢ × ▢

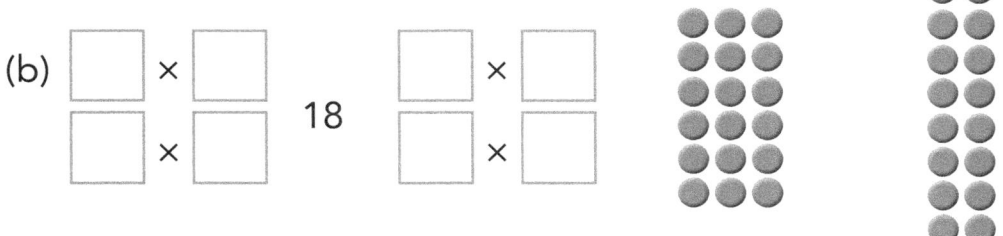

(c) ▢ × ▢   ▢ × ▢   24   ▢ × ▢   ▢ × ▢

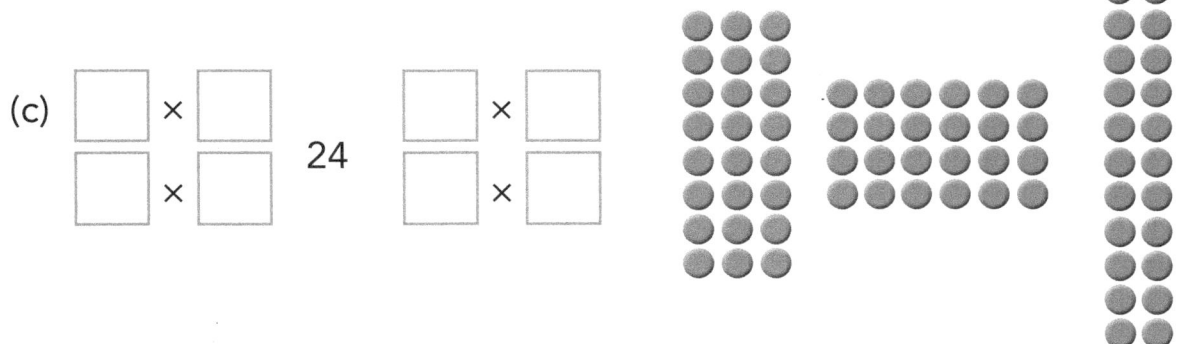

(d) ▢ × ▢   ▢ × ▢   36   ▢ × ▢   ▢ × ▢

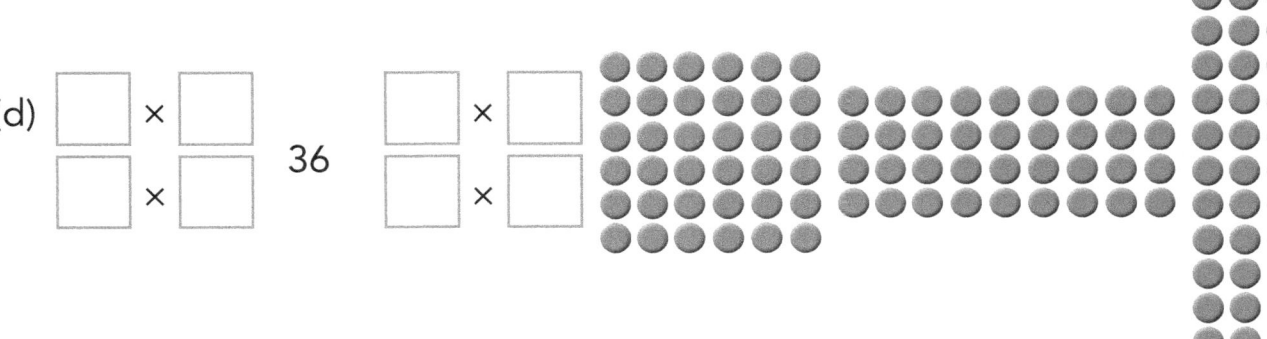

2. These are the number and types of animals in a pet shop.

| 16 rabbits | There are 8 times more mice than cats | 24 hamsters | The number of guinea pigs is half the number of rabbits. |
| 5 cats | | | |

Answer the questions. Write the number sentences and find the answers.

(a) The hamsters are kept in six cages and there is the same number of hamsters in each cage. How many hamsters are in each cage?

_____

(b) How many guinea pigs are there?

_____

(c) Each of the cats gets two tins of food a day. How many tins will be needed to feed these cats for a week?

_____

(d) There are 10 mice to a cage. How many cages are there with mice?

_____

(e) Four rabbits are kept in a hutch. Each hutch either has all males or all females.

Can you find three different numbers of male and female rabbits in the pet shop?

**Option 1**
☐ males and
☐ females

**Option 2**
☐ males and
☐ females

**Option 3**
☐ males and
☐ females

## 🚶 Shopping

There are many opportunities for quick practice of multiplying and dividing while out shopping. Ask your child questions about how many there are in different numbers of multipack foods; for example, if you have a pack of eight bread rolls, ask how many rolls there are in three packs. For the number of people in your family, ask how many pieces of fruit you need to buy for one week so that everyone has one piece of fruit each day. How many would you need if you all eat five a day? If there are large packs, such as 12 eggs, ask how many eggs each person would have if they were shared equally between your family, (look at a pack of 10 eggs if you are a family of five).

# 2.8 Posing multiplication and division questions (2)

## Write multiplication and division number sentences

1. Answer these.
   (a) I'm thinking of a number. If I divide it by 3, the answer is 6.
   What is my number? ☐
   
   (b) I'm thinking of a number. If I multiply it by 4, the answer is 32.
   What is my number? ☐
   
   (c) I'm thinking of a number. If I divide it by 5, the answer is 10.
   What is my number? ☐
   
   (d) I'm thinking of a number. If I multiply it by 9, the answer is 54.
   What is my number? ☐

2. Answer these problems.
   (a) Ajay built a tall tower of bricks until the last 7 bricks broke off in one piece. The remaining tower is 4 times the height of the piece that broke off.
   How many bricks are there in the tower now? ☐
   How many bricks high was the tower before it broke? ☐
   
   (b) After a party Freddie washed up 8 plates, then he washed the same number of cups, bowls and spoons. How many items did he wash up altogether? ☐
   
   (c) On a bus there were 5 people standing and 9 times as many people sitting down. How many people were on the bus altogether? ☐
   
   (d) Jo, her mum and two brothers bought lunch that cost £24. Their meals were the same price, how much did each lunch cost? ☐
   
   (e) Ben baked 20 flapjacks. He put half in the freezer and shared the remaining between 5 bags. How many did he put in each bag? ☐

 **Down from 60**

Play this game in pairs.

You will need: a dice, paper.

- Each player writes the number 60 at the top of a piece of paper.
- Take turns to roll a dice.
- Divide 60 by the dice number rolled. Write the answer below the 60.
- Roll the dice again. If the number rolled can divide exactly into the number written, write the answer below it.
- If the number cannot be divided exactly, pass the dice over to the other player.
- Keep going, writing each answer. The winner is the first player to reach 1.

# 2.9 Using multiplication and addition to express a number

## Solve problems involving multiplication and addition

1. Fill in the boxes.

   (a) 23 = 3 × ☐ + 2

   23 = 4 × ☐ + 3

   23 = 5 × ☐ + 3

   23 = 6 × ☐ + 5

   23 = 7 × ☐ + 2

   23 = 8 × ☐ + 7

   (b) 34 = 6 × 5 + ☐

   34 = 7 × 4 + ☐

   34 = 8 × 4 + ☐

   34 = 9 × 3 + ☐

   34 = 10 × 3 + ☐

   34 = 11 × 3 + ☐

2. Look at the score on this Target Board.

   This score is 36.

   8 × 2 = 16

   10 × 2 = 20

   Total ⟶ 36

   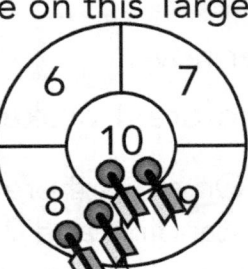

   Write these total scores.

   (a) 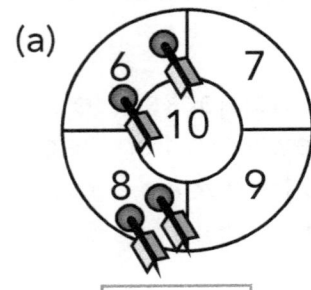  ☐

   (b) 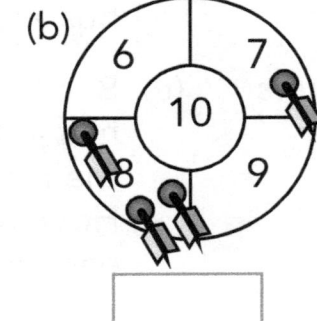  ☐

   (c) 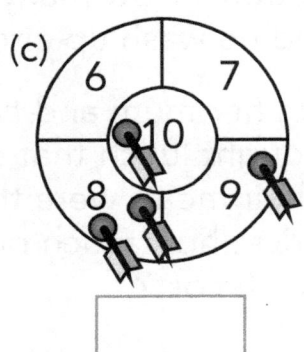  ☐

   Investigate the different totals you can make on this Target Board with five darts.

## Target board

Make your own Target Board from card like the one for Question 2. You can put your own numbers in or use 6, 7, 8, 9 and 10.

**You will need:** card, scrunched up balls of paper.

Play a game in pairs to try to get the highest score. Place the Target Board on the floor and stand over it, with five small rolled up pieces of paper as the 'darts'. Drop one dart at a time on to the board and work out your total. Keep a record of your scores and see who has the highest total after three rounds.

# 2.10 Division with a remainder

## Understand remainders in division as leftovers

1. Circle the sandwiches in groups and write number sentences.

   (a)

   There are ☐ groups.
   There are ☐ left over.
   16 ÷ ☐ = ☐ r ☐

   (b)

   There are ☐ groups.
   There are ☐ left over.
   16 ÷ ☐ = ☐ r ☐

2. Complete these.

   (a) 32 ÷ 5 = ☐ r ☐
   (b) 25 ÷ 3 = ☐ r ☐
   (c) 43 ÷ 8 = ☐ r ☐
   (d) 52 ÷ 7 = ☐ r ☐

3. Answer these problems.

   Kay shared a bag of sweets with 2 friends.
   They each got 6 sweets and there were 2 left over.
   How many were there in the bag altogether? ☐

## Remainders

**You will need:** counters and dice.

Play this game in pairs. Each write the numbers 0, 1, 2, 3 and 4 on a piece of paper. Put about 20 counters in a box and take turns to take out a large handful – this is the dividend (the number that is being divided). Roll the dice and this is the divisor (the number the dividend is being divided by).

Work out the quotient (the answer) and then cross out the written number that matches the remainder.

Example:

14 counters are taken out and a 3 is rolled with the dice.

14 ÷ 3 = 4 remainder 2. Cross out the 2 written on the paper.

Continue this until one of you crosses out all five numbers. They are the winner.

©HarperCollinsPublishers 2018

# 2.11 Calculation of division with a remainder (1)

## Solve division problems with remainders

**1.** James shares everything equally between himself and three friends. How many will they each get? How many will be left over?

(a)

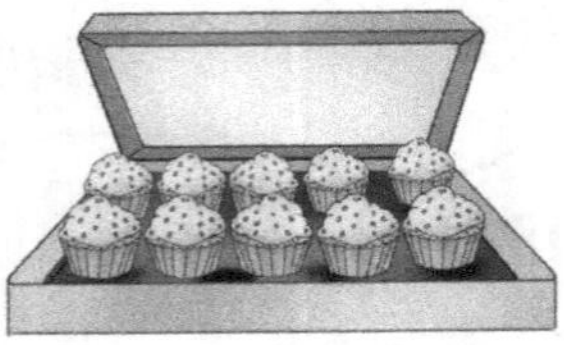

$10 \div 4 =$ ☐ r ☐

(b)

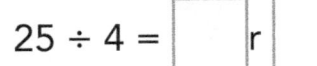

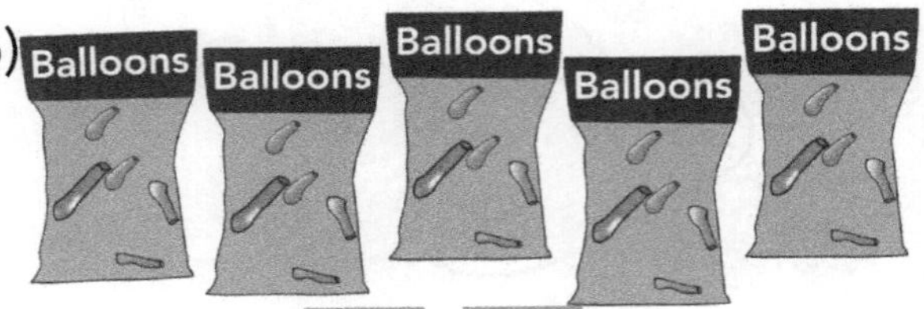


$25 \div 4 =$ ☐ r ☐

(c)

$18 \div 4 =$ ☐ r ☐

(d)

$15 \div 4 =$ ☐ r ☐

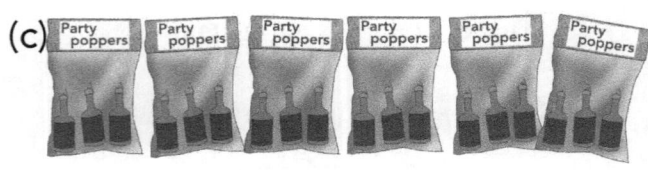

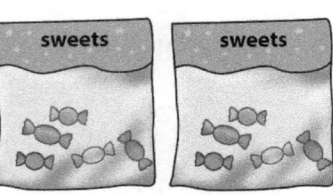

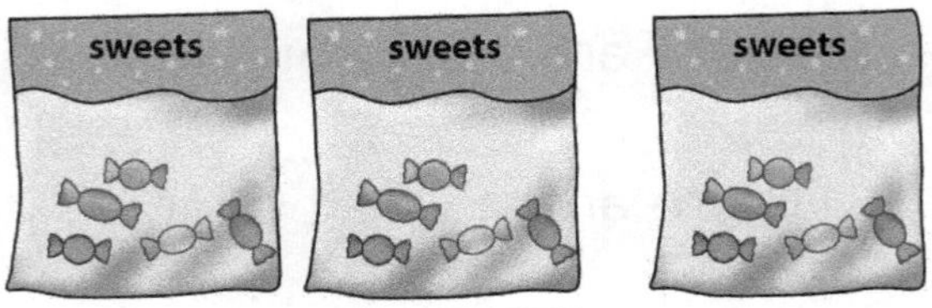

**2.** What is the greatest number you can put in each box?

(a) $6 \times$ ☐ $< 55$ (b) $7 \times$ ☐ $< 41$ (c) $5 \times$ ☐ $< 27$

(d) ☐ $\times 9 < 22$ (e) $8 \times$ ☐ $< 60$ (f) ☐ $\times 8 < 38$

**3.** Answer these problems.

(a) Tables are made with 4 legs each. A carpenter has 35 legs. How many tables can be made? How many legs will be left over? ☐

(b) There are 30 days in June. How many weeks plus how many days are there in June? ☐

## Remainder 1

Use multiplication and division facts your child knows to work out divisions that leave a remainder of 1. Work them out in these stages:

**1.** Multiplication $4 \times 5 = 20$

**2.** Division $20 \div 5 = 4$

**3.** Remainder of 1 $21 \div 5 = 4$ r $1$

Ask your child to try to make up two division calculations that leave a remainder of 1.


©HarperCollins*Publishers* 2018

# 2.12 Calculation of division with a remainder (2)

## Solve division problems with remainders

1. Write the missing numbers.

   (a) ☐ ÷ 3 = 4 r 2   (b) ☐ ÷ 9 = 3 r 6

   (c) ☐ ÷ 6 = 7 r 1   (d) ☐ ÷ 4 = 8 r 2

   (e) ☐ ÷ 5 = 5 r 4   (f) ☐ ÷ 10 = 7 r 8

2. Fill in the boxes to show each number sentence.

   (a) A teacher puts 9 books on 5 shelves, but still has 3 books left over. How many books does the teacher have altogether?

   (b) When 7 packs of counters are shared into sets of 6, there are 3 counters left over. How many counters are there altogether?

   ☐ × ☐ + ☐ = ☐          ☐ × ☐ + ☐ = ☐

3. Use these number sentences to write divisions with remainders.

   (a) 5 × 4 + 3 = 23   (b) 3 × 6 + 2 = 20

   23 ÷ ☐ = 4 r ☐        ☐ ÷ 3 = ☐ r ☐

   23 ÷ ☐ = 5 r ☐        ☐ ÷ 6 = ☐ r ☐

   (c) 8 × 3 + 1 = 25   (d) 4 × 9 + 3 = 39

   25 ÷ ☐ = ☐ r ☐        ☐ ÷ ☐ = ☐ r ☐

   25 ÷ ☐ = ☐ r ☐        ☐ ÷ ☐ = ☐ r ☐

## Multiplying and dividing

Look at each of the questions above and ask your child about the way in which multiplication and division are linked. For Question 1, encourage them to leave the remainders until later in the calculation and then multiply together the other two numbers. They can then add the remainder. Once completed, go back through it, dividing it to see how it relates to the multiplication fact.

Questions 2 and 3 start from a multiplication, so reinforce the link between that and division.

# 2.13 Calculation of division with a remainder (3)

## Solve division problems with remainders

1. This calculation will leave a remainder. What is the greatest possible dividend? What is the lowest possible dividend?

   ● ÷ 3 = 7 r ☐

   The greatest possible number for the ● is ☐.

   The lowest possible number for the ● is ☐.

2. Look at these. The number in the ● is the same for each division.

   ● ÷ 2 = ▲ r 1     ● ÷ 3 = ▲ r 1     ● ÷ 4 = ▲ r 1

   What is the lowest possible missing number? Complete these:

   (a) ☐ ÷ 2 = ☐ r 1    (b) ☐ ÷ 3 = ☐ r 1    (c) ☐ ÷ 4 = ☐ r 1

3. Answer these.

   (a) At a party there are 22 children. Balloons are sold in packs of 8. How many packs of balloons are needed so that every child gets a balloon each? ☐

   (b) Envelopes are sold in packs of 6 and a business needs to post 34 letters. How many packs of envelopes are needed to have an envelope for every letter? ☐

---

### 👪 Division problems

Question 3 has problems that your child may find difficult, as they need to interpret the question and put it into a real context. They may wish to use practical objects or draw pictures to show each division, to help them decide whether they need to make the answer higher or lower to answer the problem correctly. Always read back through the problem to see if the answer actually solves the problem.

# 3.1 Knowing numbers up to 1000 (1)

## Read, write and partition numbers up to 1000

1. Look at the diagrams and write each number.

   Example: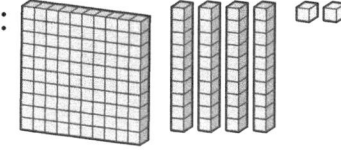

   In numerals: 142

   In words: one hundred and forty-two

   (a)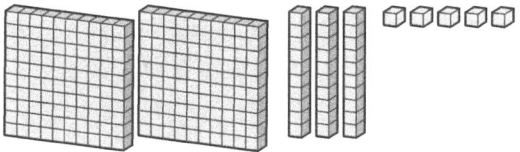

   In numerals: _____

   In words: _____

   (b)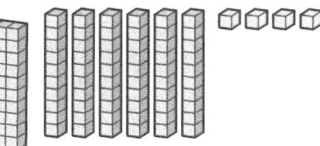

   In numerals: _____

   In words: _____

   (c)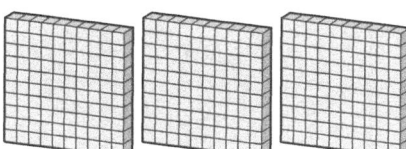

   In numerals: _____

   In words: _____

   (d)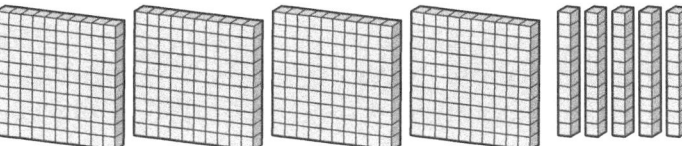

   In numerals: _____

   In words: _____

2. Write how many hundreds, tens and ones there are in each of these 3-digit numbers.

| Hundreds | Tens | Ones |
|---|---|---|
|  | | |

(a) 334 = ☐ hundreds + ☐ tens + ☐ ones

| Hundreds | Tens | Ones |
|---|---|---|
| 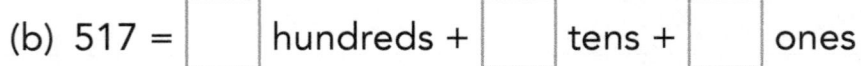 | | |

(b) 517 = ☐ hundreds + ☐ tens + ☐ ones

| Hundreds | Tens | Ones |
|---|---|---|
| 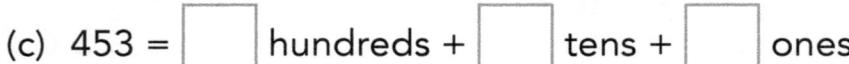 | | |

(c) 453 = ☐ hundreds + ☐ tens + ☐ ones

| Hundreds | Tens | Ones |
|---|---|---|
| | | |

(d) 621 = ☐ hundreds + ☐ tens + ☐ ones

# Partitioning numbers

Partitioning numbers involves breaking them up into separate parts. We often partition numbers into hundreds, tens and ones, so, for example the number 456 could be partitioned into 400 + 50 + 6. Being able to do this confidently helps to understand the value of the number and is useful when it comes to calculating with larger numbers.

When you are out and about with your child or at home, encourage your child to try to spot numbers they see and say them aloud. They can then try to partition the numbers into hundreds, tens and ones.

# 3.2 Knowing numbers up to 1000 (2)
## Place value of numbers up to 1000

1. Write the missing numbers or words to complete each of these.

    (a) 739 ⟶ _____

    (b) [ ] ⟶ two hundred and fifty-seven

    (c) 414 ⟶ _____

    (d) [ ] ⟶ eight hundred and forty

2. Draw diagrams to represent the numbers and then write them as numerals.

| Number | Drawing | Numeral |
|---|---|---|
| Three hundred and forty-two | | 342 |
| (a) Two hundred and eighty | | |
| (b) Four hundred and twenty-five | | |

3. Circle the digit in each number that represents these values.

    (a) Which digit represents seven hundred? ...... 7 7 7

    (b) Which digit represents 80? .................. 8 8 8

    (c) Which digit represents four? ................ 4 4 4

### Place value pick-up

You will need: number cards 1–9.

Use a set of 1–9 number cards; shuffle and place the cards face down. You and your child each choose any three cards and make the largest possible number by placing them next to each other. For example, the largest possible number with the digits 2, 8 and 5 is 852. The person with the largest number wins a point and the winner is the first to collect 10 points. Repeat and make the smallest possible number with the three cards.

©HarperCollinsPublishers 2018

# 3.3 Number lines (to 1000) (1)

## Compare and order numbers up to 1000

1. Write the number that each letter is pointing to.

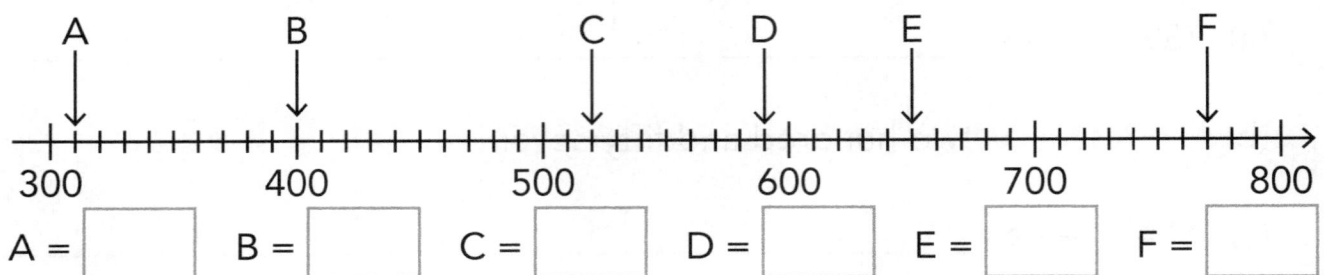

A = ☐   B = ☐   C = ☐   D = ☐   E = ☐   F = ☐

2. Draw an arrow and write each letter at the correct number on the number line.

   A = 671    B = 680    C = 695    D = 704    E = 718    F = 722

3. Count and complete the number patterns.

   (a) 236, 237, 238, ☐, ☐, 241

   (b) 580, 590, 600, ☐, ☐, 630

   (c) 992, 991, 990, ☐, ☐, 987

   (d) 450, ☐, ☐, 600, 650, 700

4. Put these numbers in order. Start from the greatest.

   600    389    471    630    87    390    409    742

   ☐ > ☐ > ☐ > ☐ > ☐ > ☐ > ☐ > ☐

 Ordering numbers

Look at the mass in grams of different cans and packets in your cupboards. Choose a selection that have a total mass of up to 1 kg, measured in grams. Ask your child to read each of the amounts, saying each number aloud, and then put them in order, starting with the heaviest.

For more of a challenge, they could try to estimate the mass of each can or packet and put them into an order. This can then be checked against the actual order after reading each amount.

# 3.4 Number lines (to 1000) (2)
## Compare and order numbers up to 1000

1. Draw an arrow and write each letter at the correct position on the number line

   A = 377    B = 384    C = 390    D = 406    E = 412    F = 421

2. Complete these number patterns.

   (a) ☐, ☐, 518, 520, 522, ☐    (b) ☐, 345, 350, 355, ☐, ☐

   (c) 462, ☐, 662, 762, ☐, ☐    (d) 875, 895, 915, ☐, ☐, ☐

3. Compare the numbers. Write >, < or = in the ◯.

   (a) 131 ◯ 113    (b) 904 ◯ 940
   (c) 667 ◯ 766    (d) 585 ◯ 582
   (e) 252 ◯ 252    (f) 401 ◯ 399
   (g) 300 + 60 + 4 ◯ 346    (h) 803 ◯ 800 + 30

4. What is the greatest digit you can write in the box for each number statement to be true?

   (a) ☐12 < 821    (b) 4☐5 > 465    (c) 453 < 45☐
   (d) 766 > ☐76    (e) 242 > ☐39    (f) 79☐ < 798

---

### 👪 Comparing numbers

The symbols <, > and = are used to compare numbers, to show which is greater or smaller or whether they are equal.

Make sure your child recognises the signs and can distinguish between < and >. A good way to learn this is to draw a large set of the symbols and to put building bricks or counters in place, with the larger number in the open end of the < and > symbols. Practise this with different numbers.

< means 'is less than'
> means 'is more than'
= means 'is equal to'

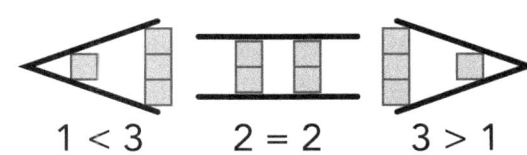

1 < 3    2 = 2    3 > 1

©HarperCollinsPublishers 2018

# 3.5 Fun with the place value chart (1)

## Place value of numbers up to 1000

1. Look at the diagrams and say each number aloud. Write each number.

   (a) 
   | Hundreds | Tens | Ones |
   |---|---|---|
   | ● ● ● ● | ● ● | ● ● ● |

   In numerals: ☐

   (b)
   | Hundreds | Tens | Ones |
   |---|---|---|
   |  | ● ● ● | ● ● ● |

   In numerals: ☐

   (c)
   | Hundreds | Tens | Ones |
   |---|---|---|
   | ● ● ● ● ● ● |  | ● ● ● ● |

   In numerals: ☐

   (d)
   | Hundreds | Tens | Ones |
   |---|---|---|
   |  | ● | ● ● ● |

   In numerals: ☐

2. Draw dots to represent each number.

   (a) 406
   | Hundreds | Tens | Ones |
   |---|---|---|
   |  |  |  |

   (b) 630
   | Hundreds | Tens | Ones |
   |---|---|---|
   |  |  |  |

   (c) 500
   | Hundreds | Tens | Ones |
   |---|---|---|
   |  |  |  |

   (d) 362
   | Hundreds | Tens | Ones |
   |---|---|---|
   |  |  |  |

3. Ben has drawn dots in the place value chart to show 436. Sonia draws one more dot. What might the new number be? There are three possibilities.

   | Hundreds | Tens | Ones |
   |---|---|---|
   | ● ● ● ● | ● ● ● | ● ● ● ● ● ● |

   | Hundreds | Tens | Ones |
   |---|---|---|
   |  |  |  |

   | Hundreds | Tens | Ones |
   |---|---|---|
   |  |  |  |

   | Hundreds | Tens | Ones |
   |---|---|---|
   |  |  |  |

   In numerals: _____   In numerals: _____   In numerals: _____

---

 **Place value charts**

When using place value charts, make sure your child sees the value of the dots in each column. For example, for Question 3, there are 4 hundreds, 3 tens and 6 ones. This shows that 400 + 30 + 6 = 436.

**You will need:** number cards 0–9, counters.

# 3.6 Fun with the place value chart (2)

## Place value of numbers up to 1000

1. Draw four dots in the place value charts below to represent six different 3-digit numbers. Write each number in words.

| Hundreds | Tens | Ones |
|---|---|---|
|  |  |  |

In words: _____

| Hundreds | Tens | Ones |
|---|---|---|
|  |  |  |

In words: _____

| Hundreds | Tens | Ones |
|---|---|---|
|  |  |  |

In words: _____

| Hundreds | Tens | Ones |
|---|---|---|
|  |  |  |

In words: _____

2. Draw dots in the top place value chart to represent 347. Then, in each chart below, move one dot into another column and write the number.

| Hundreds | Tens | Ones |
|---|---|---|
|  |  |  |

| Hundreds | Tens | Ones |
|---|---|---|
|  |  |  |

In words: _____

In numerals: ☐

| Hundreds | Tens | Ones |
|---|---|---|
|  |  |  |

In words: _____

In numerals: ☐

 **Place value charts**

For Question 1 there are 15 possible numbers that can be made with four dots. As a challenge your child could try to find all 15 of them. Encourage them to be systematic so they find all the possibilities. They could start with the largest possible number (400) and get smaller one number at a time (310, 301, 220, 211, 202, …). They may choose their own way of finding all the numbers.

If you want to help them become more systematic, try starting with just one dot. This gives three possible numbers: 100, 10 and 1. Then go on to two dots and they should find that this gives six possible numbers. They could then try three dots, then four, so that they become more skilled at finding all the possible numbers.

# 4.1 From statistical tables to bar charts

## Interpret and represent data using tables and bar charts

**1.** Read the bar chart and then complete the statistical table.

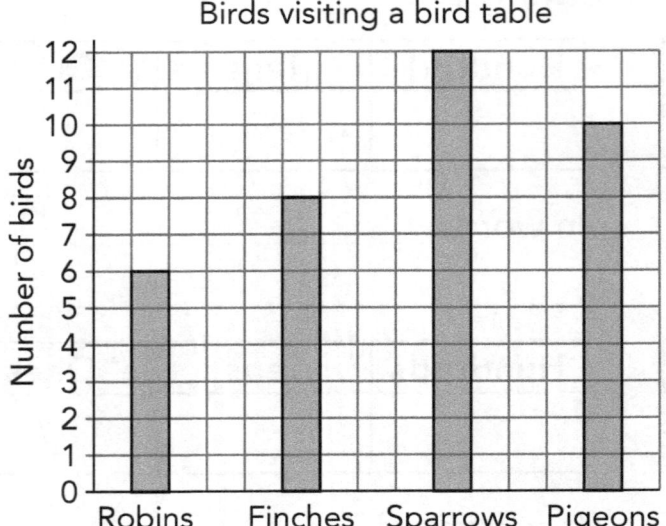

| Type of bird | Number of birds |
|---|---|
| Robins | |
| Finches | |
| Sparrows | |
| Pigeons | |

**2.** This table shows the number of children in a school born in each month from January to June. Use these results to complete the bar chart.

| January | February | March | April | May | June |
|---|---|---|---|---|---|
| 6 | 5 | 10 | 2 | 4 | 12 |

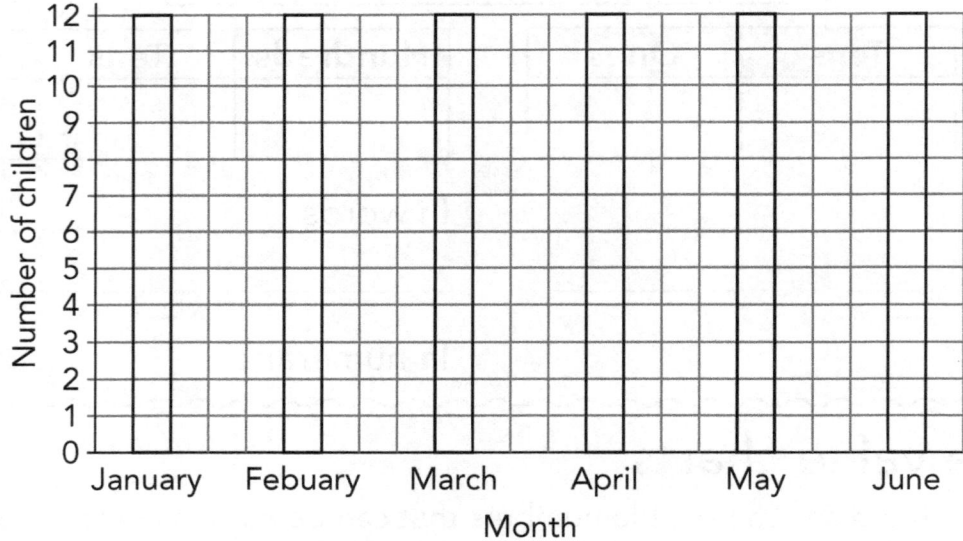

## Collecting data

Record things around you, such as the number of each type of bird you see outside, colours of cars, or type of fruit you have at home. To record information, use a tally chart. Remind your child that 5 is shown as 𝍸. Count up the total of tallies for each group and write them in a table.


©HarperCollins*Publishers* 2018

# 4.2 Bar charts (1)

## Interpret and represent data using bar charts

1. Each week Emma has a spelling test, with 20 words to learn for each test. This table shows her results for 6 weeks.

| Week 1 | Week 2 | Week 3 | Week 4 | Week 5 | Week 6 |
|---|---|---|---|---|---|
| 18 | 14 | 13 | 11 | 17 | 19 |

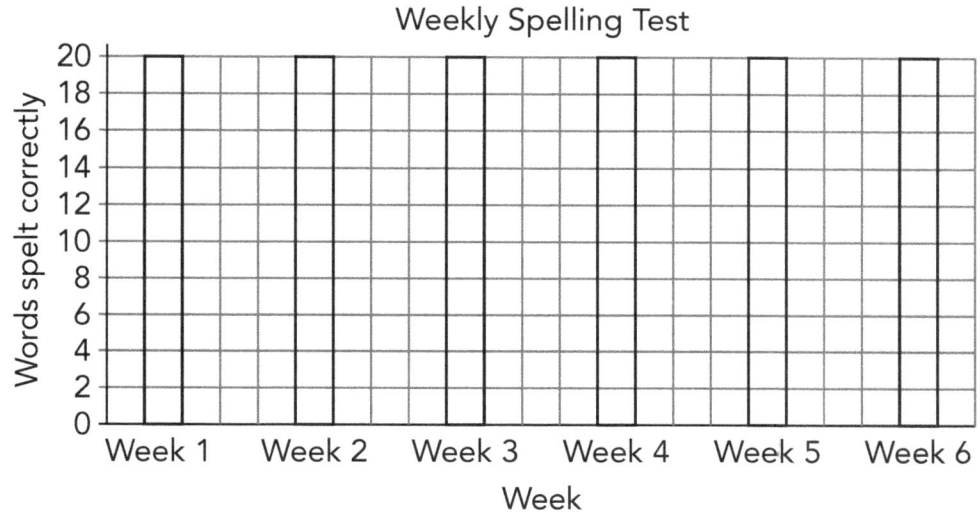

(a) Draw the bar chart from the information in the table.
(b) How many words did she spell correctly in Week 3?

_____

(c) In which week did she score 11 out of 20?

_____

(d) In which week did she make two mistakes with her spellings?

_____

(e) How many more words did she spell correctly in Week 6 than in Week 2?

_____

## 👪 Bar charts

**You will need:** objects that can be sorted by colour, a large sheet of plain paper, graph paper.

Start with a collection of objects of different colours such as toy cars, a handful of building bricks, crayons or socks. Sort the objects by colour into columns. Write how many of each object in a table. Draw columns like a bar graph on a large piece of paper. Write 'Colour' as the title underneath and write a different colour beneath each column. At the side, write 'Number of … (cars/bricks/socks)' and write the numbers 0–8 at the side of the chart, evenly spaced and large enough to fit the objects. Now place the objects in each column, making sure they are in line so two or three in each column are level to match the numbers at the side. Finally, use squared paper and draw this information on to a graph with a shaded square representing each item.

# 4.3 Bar charts (2)

## Interpret and represent data using tables, pictograms and bar charts

1. These are the number of ice creams sold by a cafe each day in one week.

| Mon | Tues | Weds | Thurs | Fri | Sat | Sun |
|---|---|---|---|---|---|---|
| 8 | 5 | 8 | 3 | 7 | 11 | 9 |

This can be shown as a pictogram.

**Daily ice-cream sales**

| Mon | ▲▲▲▲ |
| Tues | ▲▲▴ |
| Weds | ▲▲▲▲ |
| Thurs | ▲▴ |
| Fri | ▲▲▲▴ |
| Sat | ▲▲▲▲▲▴ |
| Sun | ▲▲▲▴ |

Key  ▲ = 2 ice-creams
     ▴ = 1 ice-cream

(a) How many ice creams were sold on Friday?

(b) How many ice creams were sold on Monday?

(c) On which day were 9 ice creams sold? _____

(d) How many more ice creams were sold on Saturday than Thursday?

(e) On which two days were the same number of ice creams sold? _____

2. A school is collecting supermarket vouchers. The children collect their vouchers in teams, the results of which are recorded in the table below.

**Number of vouchers collected by each team**

| Team name | Ants | Bees | Moths | Wasps | Beetles |
|---|---|---|---|---|---|
| Number of vouchers | 65 | 60 | 50 | 75 | 55 |

(a) According to the results, write the teams in order, starting with the team with most vouchers.

_____

(b) Draw a bar chart based on the table.

## 👪 Reading graphs

Look at the pictogram and together with your child think of other questions that can be asked about this data, such as:

*On which day was the most ice cream sold? How many ice creams were sold altogether at the weekend? Why do you think more ice creams were sold on each day at the weekend than on midweek days?*

©HarperCollinsPublishers 2018

# 5.1 Second and minute

## Understand second and minute as units of time

1. Draw lines to match the times.

   | 1:04 | 10:57 | 3:48 | 7:19 |

2. Choose a suitable unit of time from this list to complete these sentences.

   | second | minute | hour | day | week |

   (a) Lunchtime at school lasts 1 _____.

   (b) The school summer holidays last for 6 _____.

   (c) It takes me 10 _____ to put on my coat.

   (d) My favourite song takes 3 _____ to sing.

   (e) We are at school for 5 _____ then it is the weekend.

3. Convert these times to different units.

   (a) $\frac{1}{4}$ hour = ☐ minutes       (b) 10 minutes = ☐ seconds

---

 **Timing events**

Use a clock or stopwatch to record the time taken to complete different tasks and events. Draw a table like this to record the times your child takes, encouraging them to estimate their totals before starting the timing. These are some examples; ask your child to make up their own challenges.

| Task or event | Estimate | Results |
| --- | --- | --- |
| Number of times the word minute can be written in a minute | | |
| Number of rope skips in 30 seconds | | |
| Number of minutes spent watching TV in a day | | |

# 5.2 Times on 12-hour and 24-hour clocks and in Roman numerals

## Read times in Roman numerals and convert between 12-hour and 24-hour times

1. Read the times and write them using digits.

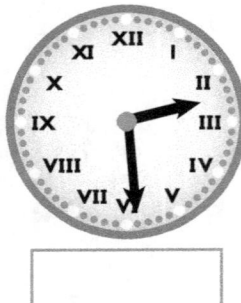 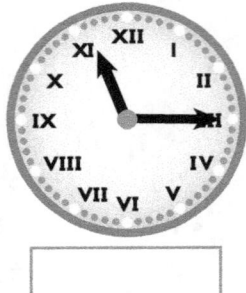 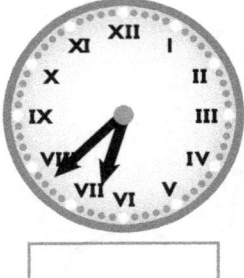 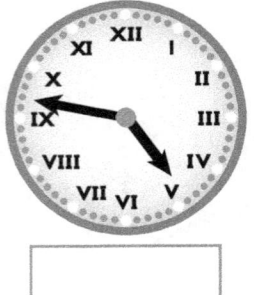

2. Complete the table for converting 12-hour time to 24-hour time.

| 12-hour time | 24-hour time |
|---|---|
|  | 02:15 |
| 5:32 a.m. |  |
|  | 23:05 |
| 8:55 p.m. |  |

| 12-hour time | 24-hour time |
|---|---|
|  | 02:20 |
| 10:20 p.m. |  |
|  | 11:14 |
| 12:45 p.m. |  |

3. Draw lines times between these three groups to match the times.

| | | |
|---|---|---|
| Seven thirty in the evening • | • 7:15 p.m. • | • 09:20 |
| Twenty past nine in the morning • | • 2:05 p.m. • | • 19:15 |
| Nine fifty-five in the evening • | • 7:30 p.m. • | • 11:15 |
| Quarter past seven at night • | • 11:15 a.m. • | • 14:05 |
| Five past two in the afternoon • | • 9:20 a.m. • | • 21:55 |
| Eleven fifteen in the morning • | • 9:55 p.m. • | • 19:30 |

 **TV times (1)**

Look at times of TV programmes for an afternoon and evening in the paper or online with your child. Ask them to write down a schedule for the start and finish times of their favourite programmes, using 24-hour clock time. Keep the table of TV times to use for Unit 5.4.

| Programme | Start time | End time |
|---|---|---|
|  |  |  |

# 5.3 Leap years and common years

## Know the number of days in each leap year and common year

1. Read and answer these.

   (a) How many minutes in one hour? _____

   (b) How many days in one week? _____

   (c) How many months in one year? _____

   (d) How many days in a common year? _____

   (e) How many days in a leap year? _____

   (f) Which year is the next leap year? _____

2. Check the calendar for next year and complete the following table.

| Month | Jan | Feb | Mar | Apr | May | June | July | Aug | Sept | Oct | Nov | Dec |
|---|---|---|---|---|---|---|---|---|---|---|---|---|
| Number of days | | | | | | | | | | | | |

   (a) There are ☐ other months with the same number of days as May.

   (b) There are ☐ other months with the same number of days as September.

   (c) There are ☐ other months with the same number of days as February.

## 👪 Days in each month

This is a good way to learn how many days there are in each month.

Put your hands together and look at your knuckles.

January is on the first knuckle of your left hand.

All the 'knuckle months' have 31 days.

February, which is the second month and so is in a space between two knuckles, has 28 days (29 days in a leap year).

The other four months have 30 days.

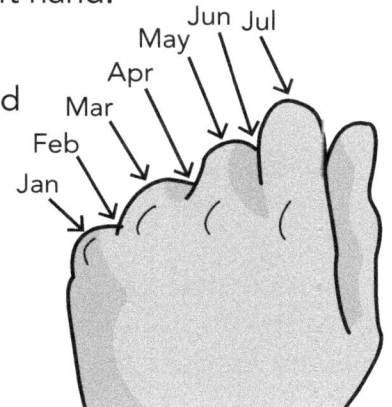

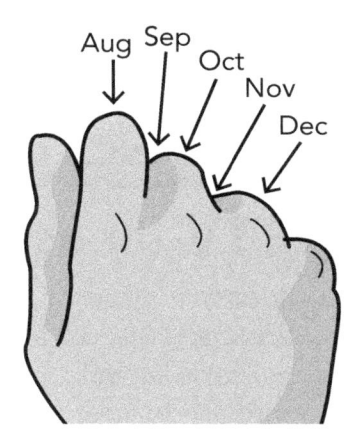

©HarperCollinsPublishers 2018

# 5.4 Calculating the duration of time

## Compare the duration of events

1. Write the difference in minutes between the times shown on the pairs of clocks.

   (a) _____ minutes

   (b) _____ minutes

   (c) _____ minutes

   (d) _____ minutes

   (e) _____ minutes

2. Read and answer these time problems.
   (a) A TV programme starts at 6:20 p.m. and lasts for half an hour. What time will it end?

   _____

   (b) Nathan gets up at 7:30 a.m. and leaves for school 55 minutes later. What time does he leave for school?

   _____

   (c) A boat leaves at 13:10 and returns later that day at 18:40. How long was the boat at sea?

   _____

   (d) A cake takes 35 minutes to bake. It is put in the oven at 17:30. When will it be ready?

   _____

   (e) Becky is playing at the park and it is 3:45 p.m. She has to go home at 4:40 p.m. How much longer does she have to play?

   _____

## TV times (2)

Look at the table of TV times recorded for Unit 5.2. At the end of each row ask your child to work out the duration of each programme from start to finish. Ask questions about the times, for example: Which is the longest programme? Which programme is the shortest? How much longer is ... than ...?

# 6.1 5 threes plus 3 threes equals 8 threes

## Solve problems involving multiplication and addition

1. Look at the pictures and complete the number sentences.
   (a) How many balls are there altogether?

   ☐ × 3 + ☐ × 3 = ☐ × 3 = ☐

   (b) How many boots are there altogether?

   ☐ × 2 + ☐ × 2 = ☐ × 2 = ☐

2. Complete these.
   (a) 3 × 5 + 2 × 5 = ☐ × 5 = ☐   (b) 2 × 6 + 8 × 6 = ☐ × 6 = ☐
   (c) 5 × 3 + 3 × 3 = ☐            (d) 6 × 5 + 3 × 5 = ☐

3. Answer these.
   (a) In a shop, all the books cost £6. Zak bought 2 books and Kim bought 3 books. How much did they spend altogether?
   
   _____
   
   (b) There are 7 books on a shelf. One cupboard has 5 shelves and the other has 4 shelves. How many books are there in total?
   
   _____

## Adding groups

Adding groups can be brought into everyday tasks. When sorting the washing, put pairs of socks that belong to each member of the family in a group. How many pairs of socks in each pile? How many individual socks altogether? If each pair of socks cost £5, how much has been spent on socks alogether? Share fruit onto plates. Decide how many plates and how many pieces of fruit are on each plate, for example six grapes and four strawberries. How many pieces of fruit are there altogether on three plates?

# 6.2 5 threes minus 3 threes equals 2 threes

## Solve problems involving multiplication and subtraction

1. Look at the pictures and complete the number sentences.
   (a) How many more fish are there than crabs?

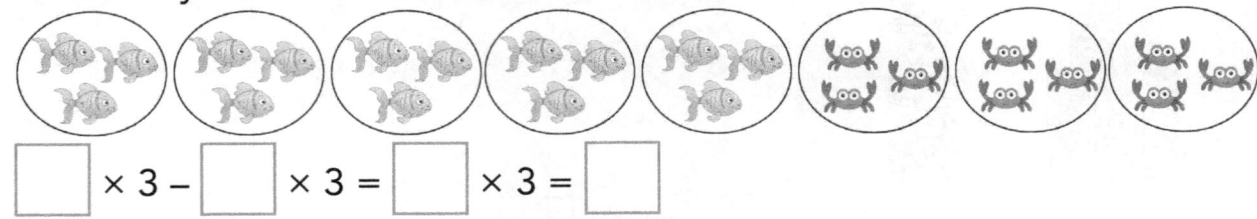

   ☐ × 3 − ☐ × 3 = ☐ × 3 = ☐

   (b) How many fewer ducks are there than frogs?

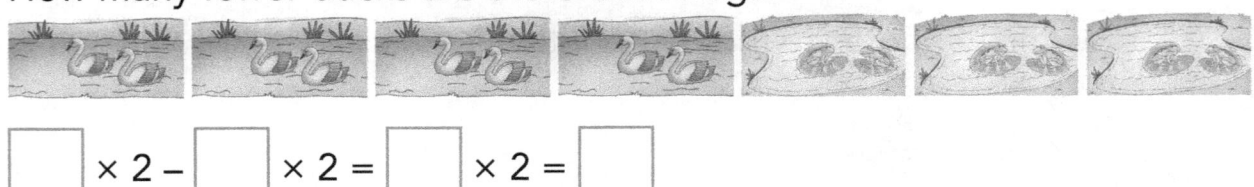

   ☐ × 2 − ☐ × 2 = ☐ × 2 = ☐

2. Complete these.
   (a) 3 × 6 − 2 × 6 = ☐ × 6 = ☐
   (b) 6 × 4 − 2 × 4 = ☐ × 4 = ☐
   (c) 8 × 5 − 3 × 5 = ☐ × 5 = ☐
   (d) 9 × 2 − 6 × 2 = ☐
   (e) 7 × 3 − 3 × 3 = ☐
   (f) 6 × 6 − 1 × 6 = ☐

3. Answer these.
   (a) Cinema tickets cost £7. The Brown family bought 4 tickets and the Green family bought 6 tickets. How much more did the Green family pay to visit the cinema than the Brown family?
   _____

   (b) Mia gives her pet rabbits 4 carrots each. There are 3 rabbits in the first hutch and 5 rabbits in the second hutch. How many more carrots did Mia put in the second hutch than the first hutch?
   _____

## Plan a party – how many more?

Look at an online shop or in a catalogue for balloons, party bags, streamers, hats, plates, napkins and any other multipack items your child chooses for a party. Find packs of different amounts, such as eight balloons and six hats, and ask, for example: If we bought three packs of each, how many more balloons would there be than hats? If the napkins are in packs of eight and plates are in packs of five, and we bought five packs of each, how many more packs of plates would be needed so there is one plate for every napkin?

# 6.3 Multiplication and division

## Use the relationship between multiplication and division to solve problems

1. Write the answers.

   (a) $3 \times 9 =$ ☐   (b) $6 \times 8 =$ ☐   (c) $5 \times 7 =$ ☐   (d) $10 \times 8 =$ ☐

   $27 \div 3 =$ ☐        $48 \div 6 =$ ☐        $35 \div 7 =$ ☐        $80 \div 10 =$ ☐

   $27 \div 9 =$ ☐        $48 \div 8 =$ ☐        $35 \div 5 =$ ☐        $80 \div 8 =$ ☐

2. What is the greatest number you can put in each box?

   (a) ☐ $\times 4 < 35$   (b) ☐ $\times 7 < 26$   (c) ☐ $\times 9 < 58$

   (d) $8 \times$ ☐ $< 40$   (e) $49 > 6 \times$ ☐   (f) $38 > 7 \times$ ☐

3. Answer these problems.
   (a) Jake has 9 pencils. He has 4 times as many crayons as pencils. How many crayons does Jake have?

   _____

   (b) A farmer collects 50 eggs on Friday and puts them into boxes that hold 6 eggs. How many full boxes of eggs will she have and how many eggs are left over?

   _____

   (c) Evie has 50 beads to make some necklaces. Tom has already made 7 necklaces and put 8 beads on each one. Who has the most beads, Evie or Tom?

   _____

   (d) There are 5 bananas in a bunch and there are 32 children in Class B. How many bunches of bananas are needed so that every child each gets a banana?

   _____

## Times towers

Use building bricks and start with a set number, such as 50. Ask your child how many towers with six bricks they think can make and how many bricks will be left over. Make the towers to check their answers. Repeat with towers of seven, eight and nine bricks.
Change the start number of bricks to 60 or 45.

**You will need:** buiding bricks.

# 6.4 Mathematics plaza – dots and patterns

## Explore patterns of odd and even numbers

1. Look at the dot patterns and write the number sentences.

   (a) 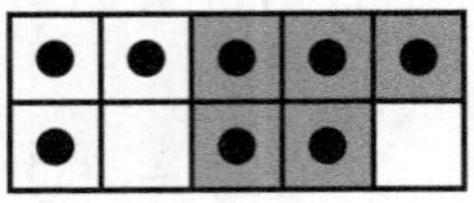 ☐ + ☐ = ☐

   (b) 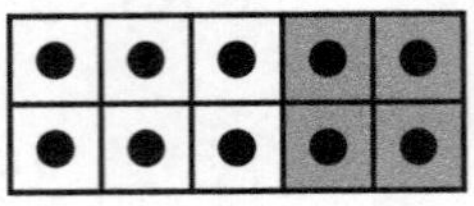 ☐ + ☐ = ☐

   (c) 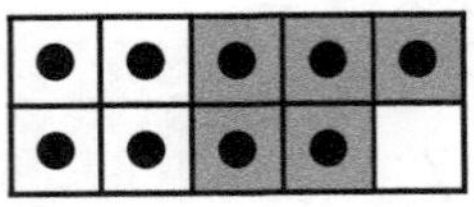 ☐ + ☐ = ☐

   (d) 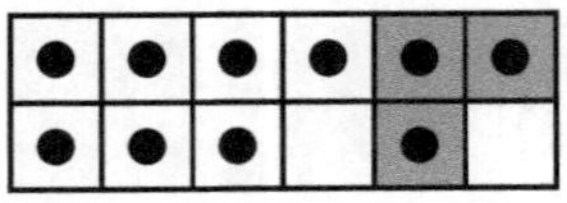 ☐ + ☐ = ☐

   (e) 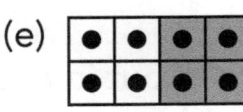 ☐ + ☐ = ☐

   (f) ☐ + ☐ = ☐

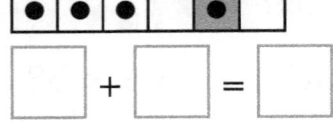

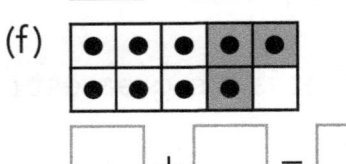

2. Write the next three numbers in these patterns.

   (a) 6, 8, 10, 12, ○, ○, ○

   (b) 9, 11, 13, 15, ○, ○, ○

   (c) 38, 36, 34, 32, ○, ○, ○

   (d) 27, 25, 23, 21, ○, ○, ○

   (e) 1, 4, 3, 6, 5, 8, ○, ○, ○

   (f) 11, 22, 33, 44, 55, 66, ○, ○, ○

3. Sort these so you have a set with odd answers and a set with even answers. Write the calculations in the diagram.

   6 + 6   3 + 4   5 + 6   5 + 5
   2 + 3   3 + 3   4 + 5   4 + 4
                   1 + 2   2 + 2

   | Odd answers | Even answers |
   |---|---|
   | 1 + 2 | |

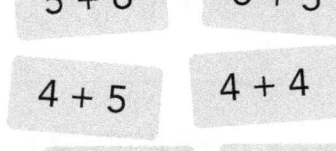

## 👪 Odds and evens

Once your child has completed Question 3, talk about the answers. What do they notice about the additions with odd answers and the additions with even answers?

**You will need:** two dice.

Play a speed game with two dice. Take turns to roll the dice and see who can shout first whether the total will be odd or even. The shout will be based on spotting if there is an odd and an even number or if there are two numbers the same, either both even or both odd. Total the dice numbers each time to check the answer.

# 6.5 Mathematics plaza – magic square

## Explore patterns on magic squares

In a magic square, each number is used once and all the numbers in every row, column and diagonal add up to the same number.

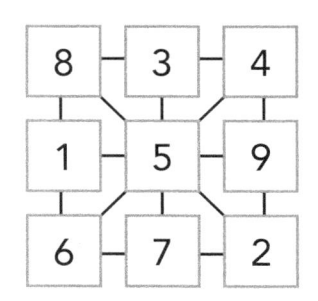

```
8 — 3 — 4
|   |   |
1 — 5 — 9
|   |   |
6 — 7 — 2
```

1. The sum of the three numbers on each line is 15. Fill in the missing numbers.

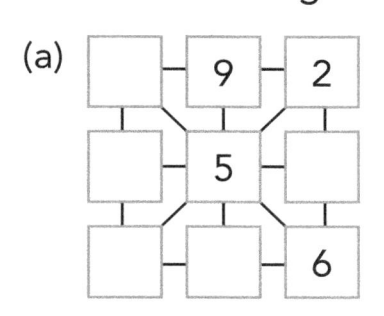

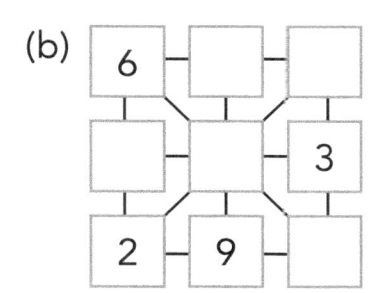

   (a) Grid with 9, 2 on top row; 5 in middle row; 6 on bottom row.

   (b) Grid with 6 on top row; 3 on middle row right; 2, 9 on bottom row.

2. Use the numbers in each set. Complete these magic squares so that they add up to the number in the circle.

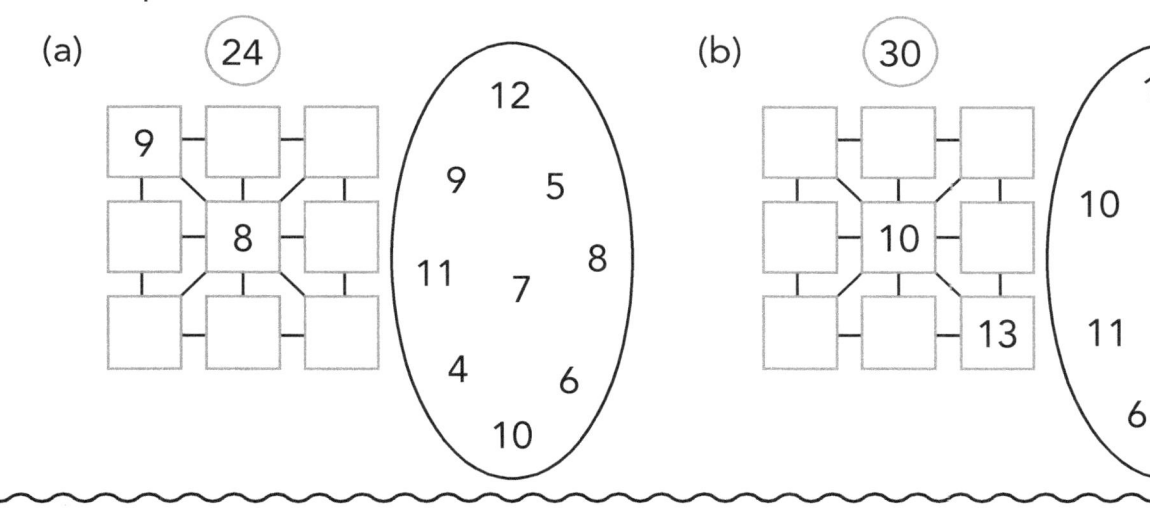

   (a) 24 — centre 8; numbers: 12, 9, 5, 8, 11, 7, 4, 6, 10; 9 given in top-left.

   (b) 30 — centre 10; numbers: 14, 7, 10, 8, 13, 11, 9, 6, 12; 10 given top middle, 13 given middle right.

---

## 👥 Magic squares

Fifteen is a common magic number total for the rows, columns and diagonals of magic squares as they use each of the numbers from 1 to 9 (see Question 1). Ask your child what they notice about the numbers opposite each other in the magic square. They should notice that all the totals are 10 (1 + 9, 2 + 8, 3 + 7, 4 + 6). The centre number, 5, is important and is the only possible position for this number to make a magic square total 15 on a 3 by 3 grid.

Look at the other examples for Question 2 with your child. Talk about the centre number and magic number total. The centre number is 8 and magic number is 24, then the centre number is 10 with a magic number of 30. Your child may notice that the magic number is always three times the centre number on a 3 by 3 magic square.

©HarperCollinsPublishers 2018

# 6.6 Numbers to 1000 and beyond

## Recognise and use place value of 3-digit and 4-digit numbers

1. Write each digit of the number in the place value chart.

    (a) 3608

    | Thousands | Hundreds | Tens | Ones |
    |---|---|---|---|
    |   |   |   |   |

    (b) 7950

    | Thousands | Hundreds | Tens | Ones |
    |---|---|---|---|
    |   |   |   |   |

    (c) 8006

    | Thousands | Hundreds | Tens | Ones |
    |---|---|---|---|
    |   |   |   |   |

    (d) 4305

    | Thousands | Hundreds | Tens | Ones |
    |---|---|---|---|
    |   |   |   |   |

2. Write the numbers represented in each place value chart.

    (a)

    | Thousands | Hundreds | Tens | Ones |
    |---|---|---|---|
    | •••• | • | •• | • |

    Written in words: _____

    Written in numerals: _____

    (b)

    | Thousands | Hundreds | Tens | Ones |
    |---|---|---|---|
    | ••• | •••••••• | | •• |

    Written in words: _____

    Written in numerals: _____

    (c)

    | Thousands | Hundreds | Tens | Ones |
    |---|---|---|---|
    | ••• | •• | ••• | •• |

    Written in words: _____

    Written in numerals: _____

    (d)

    | Thousands | Hundreds | Tens | Ones |
    |---|---|---|---|
    |   |   | •• | ••• |

    Written in words: _____

    Written in numerals: _____

## 👪 Place value arrow cards

Make a set of 12 place value arrow cards with the digits 1, 2, 3, 10, 20, 30, 100, 200, 300, 1000, 2000, 3000, like these: `3 3 3 3`

**You will need:** card, scissors.

`3 0 0 0` `3 0 0` `3 0` `3`

Together with your child, make as many different 4-digit numbers as you can with these 12 cards. Ask your child to say the number each time and record the numbers you have made.

# 6.7 Read, write and compare numbers to 1000 and beyond

## Read, write and compare numbers beyond 1000

1. Read and write these numbers in words and in numerals.

| | Write numbers in words | Write in numerals |
|---|---|---|
| (a) | two thousand five hundred and eleven | |
| (b) | seven thousand and thirty-four | |
| (c) | nine thousand eight hundred and sixty | |
| (d) | | 4972 |
| (e) | | 8103 |
| (f) | | 6015 |

2. Write in numerals the value of each digit in these numbers.

   (a) 1728 = ☐ + ☐ + ☐ + ☐

   (b) 5240 = ☐ + ☐ + ☐ + ☐

   (c) 3507 = ☐ + ☐ + ☐ + ☐

   (d) 9016 = ☐ + ☐ + ☐ + ☐

3. Write > or < in the ◯.

   (a) 147 ◯ 174     (b) 828 ◯ 282     (c) 3954 ◯ 3945

   (d) 6110 ◯ 6101   (e) 9498 ◯ 9594   (f) 7032 ◯ 3770

   (g) 3097 ◯ 3709   (h) 2646 ◯ 2466   (i) 6080 ◯ 6800

## Ordering numbers

Use the place value arrow cards you made in Unit 6.6. Remove the 2000 and 3000 cards and use the rest to make 4-digit numbers up to 2000. Record each number.

Now ask your child to write the numbers in order, starting with the smallest. Repeat this activity, removing the 200 and 300 cards and then removing the 20 and 30 cards.

©HarperCollinsPublishers 2018

# 7.1 Addition and subtraction of whole hundreds and tens (1)

## Add and subtract multiples of 10 and 100

1. Work these out mentally. Write the answers.

   (a) 3 + 4 = ☐         (b) 9 − 3 = ☐         (c) 2 + 6 = ☐
       30 + 40 = ☐           90 − 30 = ☐           20 + 60 = ☐

   (d) 8 − 4 = ☐         (e) 9 + 5 = ☐         (f) 7 − 5 = ☐
       80 − 40 = ☐           900 + 500 = ☐         700 − 500 = ☐

2. Answer these problems.
   (a) A shop orders 450 T-shirts and sells 280 in the first week. How many T-shirts are there left to sell?

   _____

   (b) Joe is counting steps. He walks 590 steps to the shop and then another 240 steps to his friend's house. How many steps has he walked in total?

   _____

   (c) Elsa's father bought a 300 cm long roll of rope. He cut off a 130 cm length and Elsa used the rest as a skipping rope. How long is Elsa's skipping rope?

   _____

   (d) Over a weekend there were 360 visitors to a museum on Saturday, which was 150 more than on Sunday. How many visitors in total went to the museum over the weekend?

   _____

## Cooking calculations

Look in recipe books or online at the weight of cooking ingredients in grams. Calculate the total weights and then you can weigh the ingredients to check your answers. Scones, biscuits and flapjack are good as they have most of the ingredients in grams. Try not to use recipes with a mix of grams and millilitres, and add 60 g for each egg. As an example, this is a recipe for shortbread: 270 g flour, 240 g butter, 90 g cornflour, 120 g sugar.

# 7.2 Addition and subtraction of whole hundreds and tens (2)

## Add and subtract multiples of 10 and 100

1. Fill in the tables.

(a)
| Addend | 350 | 410 | 240 | 370 | 290 | 360 | 430 |
|---|---|---|---|---|---|---|---|
| Addend | 120 | 290 | 340 | 260 | 320 | 450 | 390 |
| Sum | | | | | | | |

(b)
| Minuend | 140 | 230 | 280 | 510 | 630 | 570 | 650 |
|---|---|---|---|---|---|---|---|
| Subtrahend | 90 | 70 | 130 | 160 | 250 | 380 | 570 |
| Difference | | | | | | | |

2. Write the sum and the difference of the two numbers in each set.

(a) 410, 400   Sum: ____  Difference: ____

(b) 360, 90   Sum: ____  Difference: ____

(c) 600, 160   Sum: ____  Difference: ____

(d) 520, 230   Sum: ____  Difference: ____

3. Complete these diagrams. The number in a square must be the sum of the numbers on each side of it. For example: (70)—[90]—(20)

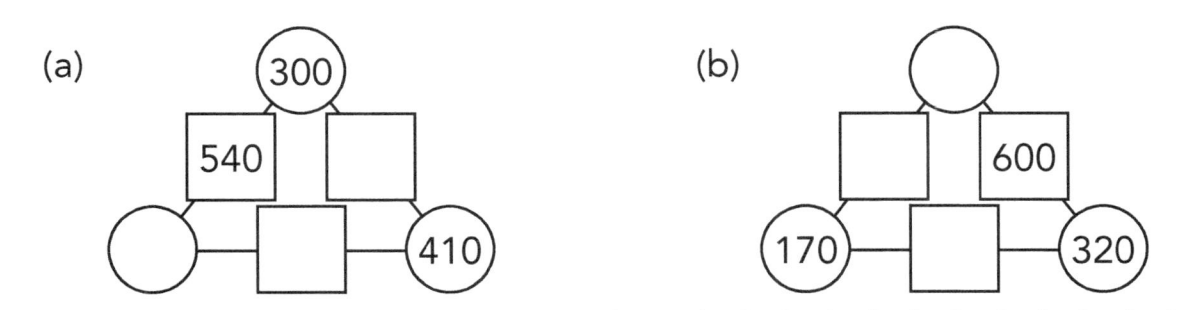

(a) top circle: 300; left square: 540; right square: ____; bottom-left circle: ____; bottom square: ____; bottom-right circle: 410

(b) top circle: ____; left square: ____; right square: 600; bottom-left circle: 170; bottom square: ____; bottom-right circle: 320

## Tiddly-wink takeaways

**You will need:** paper, tiddly-winks.

Draw a grid of 12 squares to fill the whole of a piece of paper. Write these numbers: 10, 20, 30, 40, 50, 60, 70, 80, 90, 120, 150 and 180 in each square, in any order. Think of a number over 500 that ends in zero – this is your start number. With two counters each, use one to 'ping' the other to land on the board. Taking turns, the task is to subtract the number you land on from your start number each time until you reach or go beyond zero. It can also be played to reach 500, by starting at zero and adding on each number you land on.

# 7.3 Adding and subtracting 3-digit numbers and ones (1)

## Add and subtract ones from 3-digit numbers

1. Complete these additions and subtractions on the number lines.

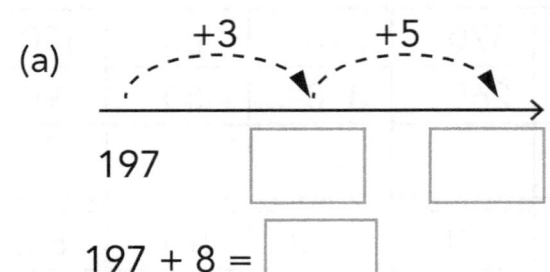

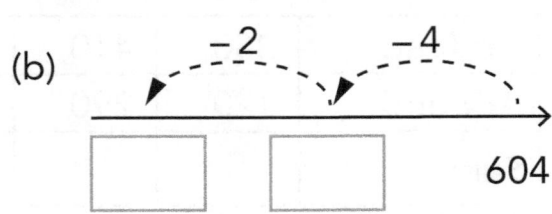

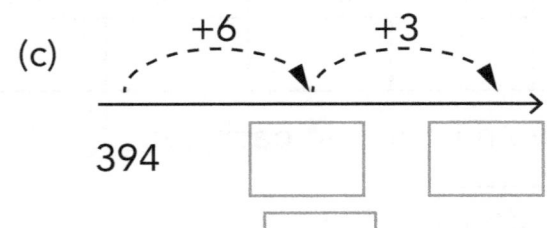

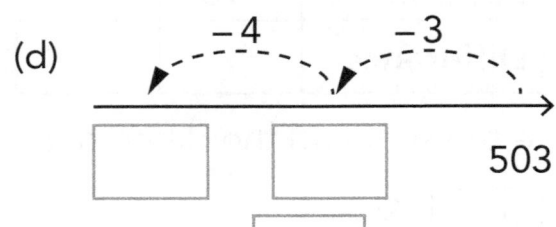

   (a) +3, +5 from 197 → ☐ → ☐

   197 + 8 = ☐

   (b) −2, −4 ending at 604: ☐ → ☐ → 604

   604 − 6 = ☐

   (c) +6, +3 from 394 → ☐ → ☐

   394 + 9 = ☐

   (d) −4, −3 ending at 503: ☐ → ☐ → 503

   503 − 7 = ☐

2. Complete each table.

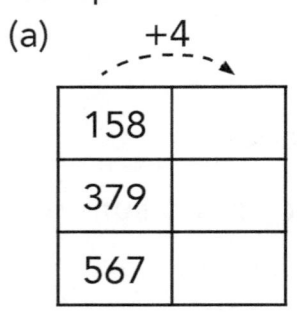

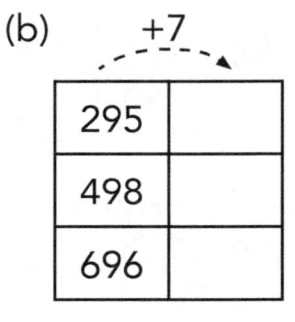

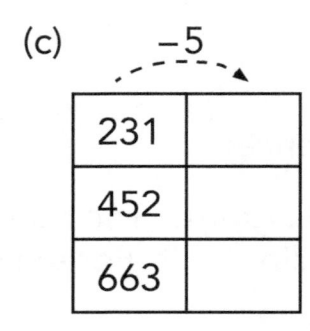

   (a) +4

   | 158 | |
   |---|---|
   | 379 | |
   | 567 | |

   (b) +7

   | 295 | |
   |---|---|
   | 498 | |
   | 696 | |

   (c) −5

   | 231 | |
   |---|---|
   | 452 | |
   | 663 | |

   (d) −8

   | 403 | |
   |---|---|
   | 506 | |
   | 702 | |

3. Calculate and then fill in each box with your answer.

   (a) 419 —+4→ ☐ —+9→ ☐ —+8→ ☐ —+7→ ☐

   (b) 256 —+6→ ☐ —−3→ ☐ —+7→ ☐ —−9→ ☐

   (c) 387 —+9→ ☐ —+5→ ☐ —−2→ ☐ —+8→ ☐

## Adders and takers

Make two sets of 1–9 number cards. Shuffle and place them face down. Turn the top three cards over in turn and write them in order to make a 3-digit number. Decide which of you will be the 'adder' or the 'taker'. Take turns to select a card; the 'adder' adds this number to the start number and the 'taker' takes away their number. Return the cards to the pile and shuffle if needed. The player who lands back on the start number is the winner.

**You will need:** two sets of number cards 1–9.

# 7.4 Adding and subtracting 3-digit numbers and ones (2)

## Add and subtract ones from 3-digit numbers

1. Complete each table.

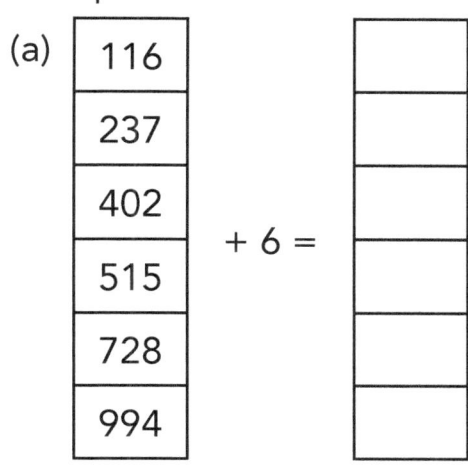

   (a)
   | | | |
   |---|---|---|
   | 116 | | |
   | 237 | | |
   | 402 | + 6 = | |
   | 515 | | |
   | 728 | | |
   | 994 | | |

   (b)
   | | | |
   |---|---|---|
   | 116 | | |
   | 237 | | |
   | 402 | − 6 = | |
   | 515 | | |
   | 728 | | |
   | 994 | | |

2. Complete each addition chart.

   (a)
   | + | 9 | 6 | 8 |
   |---|---|---|---|
   | 346 | 355 | | |
   | 298 | | | |
   | 555 | | 561 | |

   (b)
   | + | | 7 | 5 |
   |---|---|---|---|
   | 473 | | | |
   | 509 | 517 | | |
   | | | | 401 |

3. Answer these problems.
   (a) There are 185 children in Year 2. There are 6 more children in Year 3 than in Year 2. How many children are there in Year 3?

   (b) A piece of wood is 127 cm long after a carpenter cut off 8 cm. How long was the piece of wood before it was cut?

   (c) A train has 461 passengers. At the next station 5 passengers get off the train and 9 new passengers get on the train. How many passengers are there on the train now?

   (d) In a theatre my seat number is 259. My friend asks to change seats with me and I move 6 seats along. What are the two possible seat numbers I am seated at now? _____ _____

## What is my number?

Give your child some questions like these: My number is seven less than 142. What is my number? The number I am thinking of is nine more than 305. What is my number? Your child can also try to think of questions for you.

# 7.5 Addition with 3-digit numbers (1)

## Use partitioning to add 3-digit numbers

**1.** Use your preferred method to calculate these. Show your working.

(a) 541 + 265

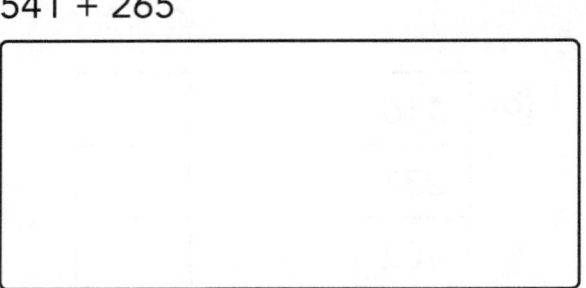

(b) 382 + 196

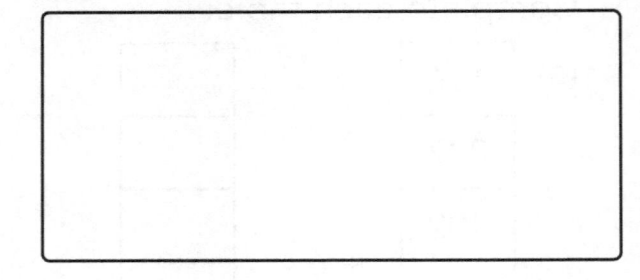

(c) 430 + 278

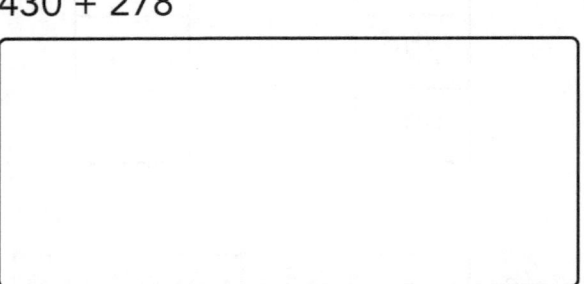

(d) 367 + 285

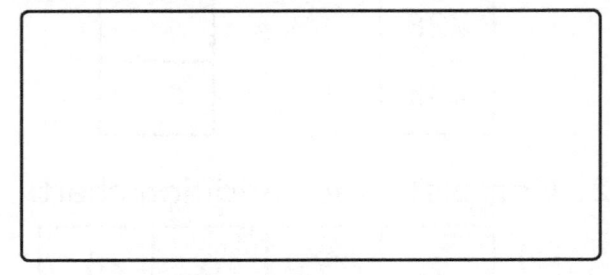

**2.** Look at these.

234 + 765 = 999

333 + 666 = 999

Find five more 3-digit additions that total 999.

## Methods and explanations

Ask your child to talk about the methods they used to answer the additions in Question 1. Did they use the same method for all four additions or did they sometimes use a different method?

When your child is finding 3-digit additions that total 999 (Question 2), ask them to say what they are thinking and to explain the method they use. Are they using their knowledge of the number bonds to 10 (1 + 9, 2 + 8, 3 + 7, 4 + 6, 5 + 5) to help with the hundreds and tens numbers?

# 7.6 Addition with 3-digit numbers (2)

**Use the column method to add 3-digit numbers**

1. Use the column method to answer these additions.

   (a)  3 5 2
      + 1 4 6

   (b)  2 0 7
      + 4 8 2

   (c)  2 3 3
      + 1 3 9

   (d)  1 7 6
      + 5 1 5

   (e)  6 4 0
      + 1 9 6

   (f)  4 8 5
      + 2 2 1

2. Read and answer these.
   (a) There are 317 children in Sahil's school and 206 children in Julia's school. How many children are there altogether?

   (b) Anna read two books each with 128 pages. How many pages did she read in total?

   (c) A taxi drives 218 km on Monday and 269 km on Tuesday. What is the total distance travelled over these two days?

3. The digits 1, 2 and 3 are missing.
   Complete these with the digits in the correct place.

   ☐ 7 ☐
   + 6 5 8
   ─────
   8 ☐ 0

## How heavy is my bag?

Choose food items from your kitchen cupboard that weigh between 50 g and 500 g, such as cereal boxes 360 g, jam 494 g. Group different pairs of items together in a bag and ask your child to calculate the total mass. Ask them to find the greatest total for any two of these items.

©HarperCollinsPublishers 2018

# 7.7 Subtraction with 3-digit numbers (1)

## Use partitioning to subtract 3-digit numbers

1. Use your preferred method to calculate these. Show your working.

    (a) 508 – 357

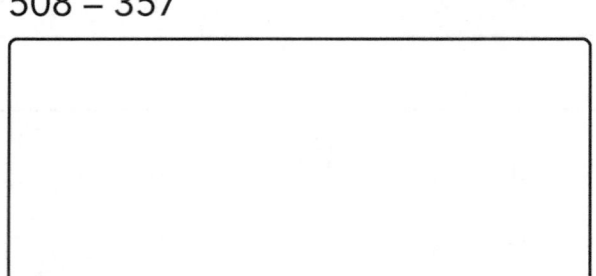

    (b) 700 – 364

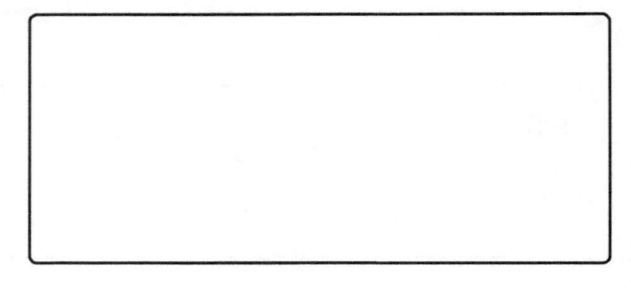

    (c) 487 – 308

    (d) 452 – 269

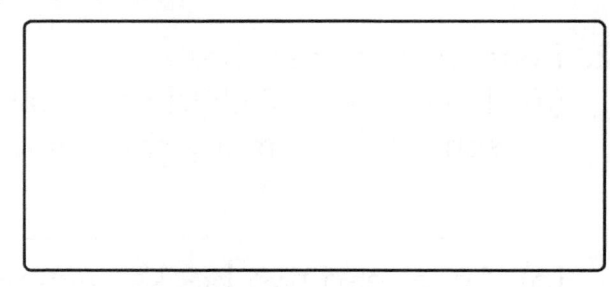

2. Look at the numbers in the stars and follow the instructions.

    759    397    426    175

    (a) Find two numbers with a difference of 333. Colour them yellow.
    (b) Find two numbers with a difference of 222. Colour them blue.
    (c) Circle the two stars with the smallest difference between them.
    (d) Find two numbers that have the largest difference. Join them with a line.

## Who's the tallest of us all?

Measure the heights of family and friends in centimetres. Write the heights in order and ask your child to find the difference between their own height and each of your friends and family. The tallest recorded man was Robert Pershing Wadlow at 272 cm. How much taller was he than your child?

Look up average heights of other things like elephants (approx. 350 cm) and compare the difference in height with Robert Pershing Wadlow or yourself. (Your child hasn't yet learned what 'average' means in maths but you can talk about 'typical' or 'usual').

# 7.8 Subtraction with 3-digit numbers (2)

## Use the column method to subtract 3-digit numbers

1. Use the column method to answer these subtractions.

   (a)  938 − 556

   (b)  762 − 349

   (c)  417 − 280

   (d)  854 − 172

   (e)  642 − 493

   (f)  530 − 186

2. Look at the prices and answer the questions.

   | ring £165 | necklace £329 | bracelet £148 | watch £257 | earrings £209 |

   (a) What is the price difference between the ring and the necklace? ☐

   (b) How much more is the cost of the watch than the bracelet? ☐

   (c) How much less does it cost to buy the earrings than the watch? ☐

   (d) What is the difference in price between the bracelet and the earrings? ☐

   (e) How much less does the ring cost than the watch? ☐

   (f) How much more is the necklace than the bracelet? ☐

## Catalogue calculating

Use a shopping catalogue or go online and let your child pretend they have £500 to spend. Which bike would they buy? How much change will they have from £500? Is there anything else they could buy with this change? How much money will they have left over now? Your child can choose different items to spend their £500 and calculate the change.

**You will need:** a shopping catalogue.

# 7.9 Estimating addition and subtraction with 3-digit numbers (1)

## Estimate and calculate the answers to addition and subtraction problems

1. Write the nearest whole tens and whole hundreds of the following numbers.

|  | 384 | 447 | 509 | 343 | 738 | 695 |
|---|---|---|---|---|---|---|
| The nearest whole ten |  |  |  |  |  |  |
| The nearest whole hundred |  |  |  |  |  |  |

2. Estimate to the nearest ten first and then calculate.

   (a) 342 + 319 = ☐     (b) 277 + 608 = ☐     (c) 425 + 334 = ☐

   Estimate: ☐           Estimate: ☐           Estimate: ☐

3. Estimate to the nearest hundred first and then calculate.

   (a) 183 + 609 = ☐     (b) 545 + 370 = ☐     (c) 253 + 335 = ☐

   Estimate: ☐           Estimate: ☐           Estimate: ☐

4. Calculate with reasoning.

   (a) 586 + 300 = ☐     (b) 700 – 540 = ☐     (c) 930 – 200 = ☐

   586 + 299 = ☐         701 – 540 = ☐         930 – 201 = ☐

   586 + 298 = ☐         702 – 540 = ☐         930 – 202 = ☐

## 👪 Bingo rounding

Make two bingo cards with six squares and write in the numbers 400, 500, 600, 700, 800 and 900. Use digit cards 0–9 (two sets if you have them), shuffle and place them face down. Take turns to select three cards each, replacing the cards and shuffling after each turn. Use the digit cards to make a 3-digit number. Round the number to the nearest hundred and cover that number on your bingo card. The first player to cover all six numbers is the winner.

**You will need:**
two sets of 0–9 number cards, card.

# 7.10 Estimating addition and subtraction with 3-digit numbers (2)

**Estimate and calculate the answers to addition and subtraction problems**

1. Calculate with reasoning. Start with the easiest calculation, so think carefully which one to start with.

    (a) 97 + 465 = ☐          (b) 550 − 97 = ☐

    98 + 465 = ☐                 550 − 98 = ☐

    99 + 465 = ☐                 550 − 99 = ☐

    100 + 465 = ☐               550 − 100 = ☐

2. Use the information to estimate the answers to the questions below.

    **Famous tall buildings throughout history**

    | Name of building | Great Pyramid of Giza | Lincoln Cathedral | Eiffel Tower | Empire State Building |
    |---|---|---|---|---|
    | Height (metres) | 146 m | 160 m | 324 m | 381 m |

    (a) About how many metres higher is Lincoln Cathedral than the Great Pyramid?  ☐ m

    (b) About how many metres shorter is the Eiffel Tower than the Empire State Building?  ☐ m

    (c) About how many metres difference is there between the Great Pyramid of Giza and the Empire State building?  ☐ m

    (d) The spire of Lincoln Cathedral collapsed over 450 years ago and today the cathedral is only 83 metres tall. About how many metres shorter is it now than it was before?  ☐ m

## Everyday numbers

Using facts and figures from information found online or in books is a useful way of practising maths skills. Make sure the numbers are in the correct range, keeping to 3-digit numbers for rounding and comparing. You can look up three distances, say between London and Cardiff, Cardiff and Glasgow and Glasgow and London. Put the facts in context to make questions, for example: If a lorry driver was driving to these places from London, about how many more miles further is it to travel to Glasgow than Cardiff?

©HarperCollinsPublishers 2018

# 8.1 Unit fractions and tenths

## Use fractions of amounts and count in tenths

1. Circle the objects in each picture to show the fraction given.
   (a)  ☆☆☆☆☆☆☆☆   $\frac{1}{4}$
   (b)  ⚾⚾⚾⚾⚾⚾⚾⚾⚾   $\frac{1}{3}$
   (c) 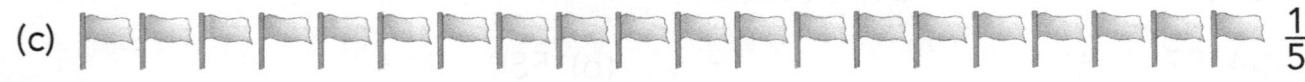 🚩🚩🚩🚩🚩🚩🚩🚩🚩🚩🚩🚩🚩🚩🚩   $\frac{1}{5}$

2. Colour these 24 balloons. 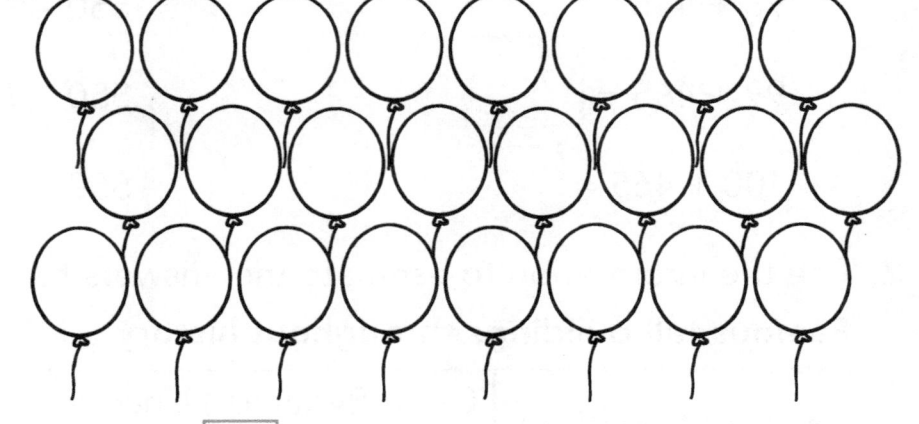
   (a) Colour $\frac{1}{6}$ blue.
   (b) Colour $\frac{1}{12}$ green.
   (c) Colour $\frac{1}{8}$ yellow.
   (d) Colour $\frac{1}{4}$ red.
   (e) Colour $\frac{1}{3}$ orange.

   How many balloons are left white? ☐

3. Write the fraction each arrow is pointing to.
   (a) Number line from 0 to 1 with marks at $\frac{1}{10}$, $\frac{2}{10}$, $\frac{3}{10}$.
   (b) Number line from 0 to 1.

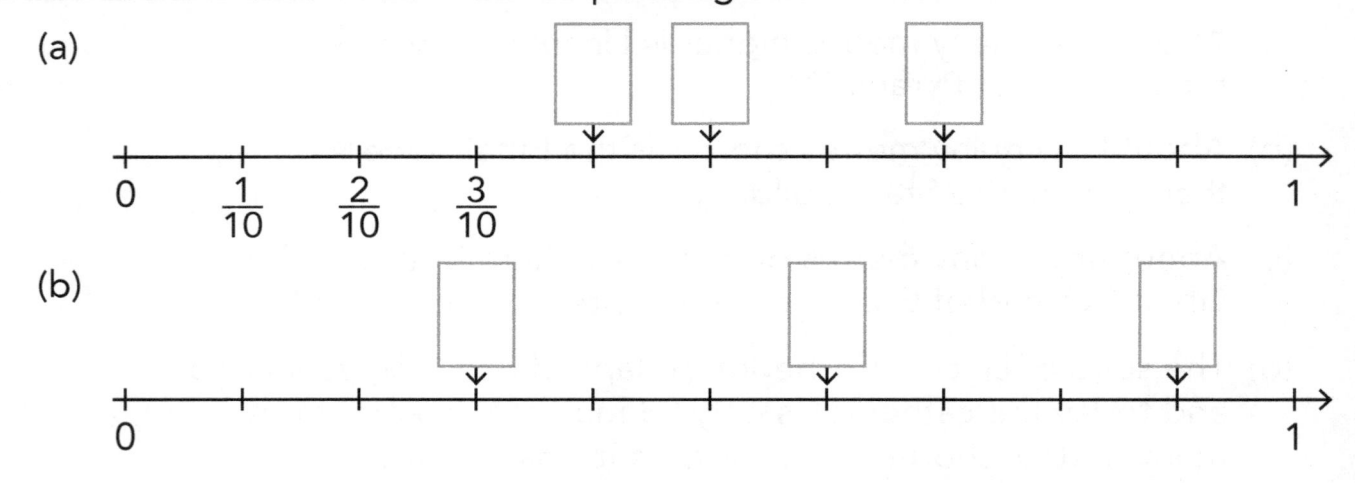

---

### 👨‍👦 Fractions of amounts

Take a look at things you have at home that can be sorted, such as crayons, packs of coloured balloons, flavoured packs of sweets, different size building bricks. Select a total of 12 or 24 and check that there are some groups (colours, flavours and so on) that make fractions such as $\frac{1}{2}, \frac{1}{4}, \frac{1}{3}, \frac{1}{6}$ ($\frac{1}{8}$ for 24 objects). Ask, for example: What fraction of crayons are green? What fractions of the sweets are strawberry? What fraction of the bricks are small? Select a total of 20 or 30 and ask your child to show you $\frac{1}{10}, \frac{2}{10}, \frac{3}{10} \ldots \frac{9}{10}$.

**You will need:** small items that can be sorted.

# 8.2 Non-unit fractions

## Use non-unit fractions of amounts

1. Look at these flags and write the fraction that is shaded.

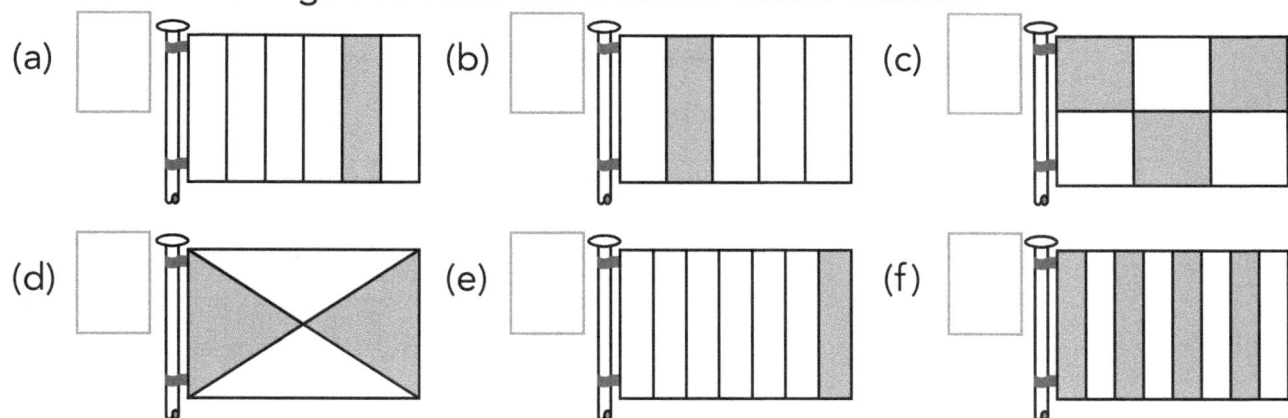

   (a) ☐   (b) ☐   (c) ☐

   (d) ☐   (e) ☐   (f) ☐

2. Design a flag with three colours in the following fractions:

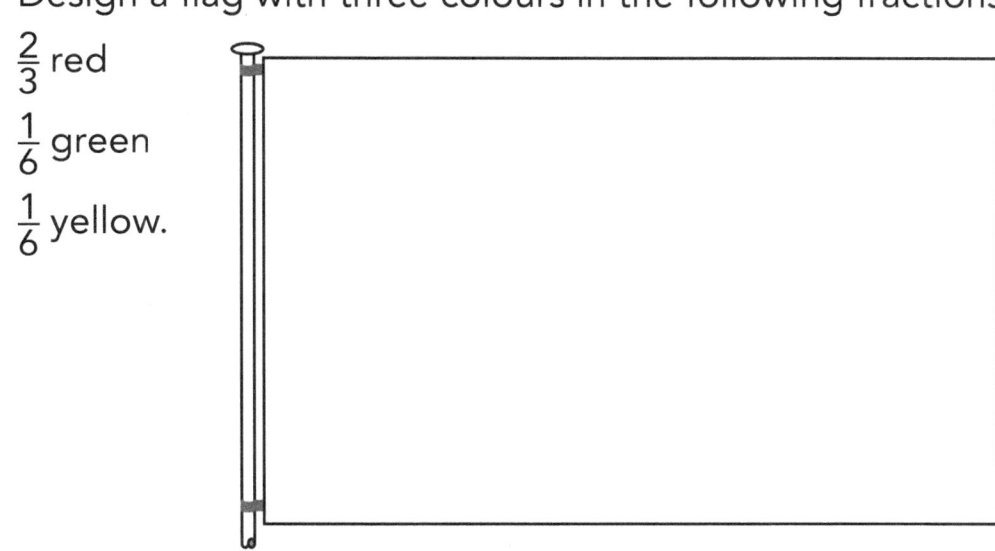

   $\frac{2}{3}$ red

   $\frac{1}{6}$ green

   $\frac{1}{6}$ yellow.

3. Put the following fractions in order, starting from the smallest.

   (a) $\frac{3}{8}$  $\frac{7}{8}$  $\frac{6}{8}$  $\frac{1}{8}$  $\frac{2}{8}$  _____

   (b) $\frac{4}{10}$  $\frac{7}{10}$  $\frac{8}{10}$  $\frac{2}{10}$  $\frac{3}{10}$  _____

### Fraction flags

On squared paper draw four rectangles the same size, 2 by 5. Ask your child to use two colours and make each rectangle into a different flag, using both colours on each. Write the fraction of each flag that is shaded in each colour (in tenths). Repeat with different groups of four flags of the same dimensions: 3 by 4, 2 by 6, 4 by 4, 5 by 3. Ask your child to write the fractions for the colours on each flag using any appropriate fractions, $\frac{2}{3}$, $\frac{1}{4}$, $\frac{3}{5}$ and so on.

**You will need:** squared paper, coloured pens or pencils.

# 8.3 Equivalent fractions

## Recognise and show equivalent fractions

1. Tick the rectangle that shows an equivalent fraction for each of these. Write each equivalent fraction.

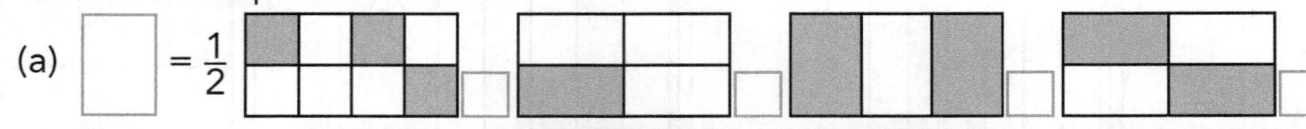

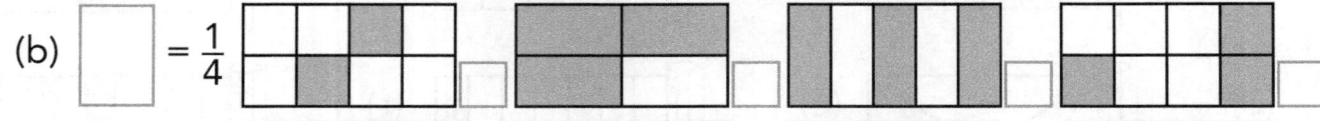

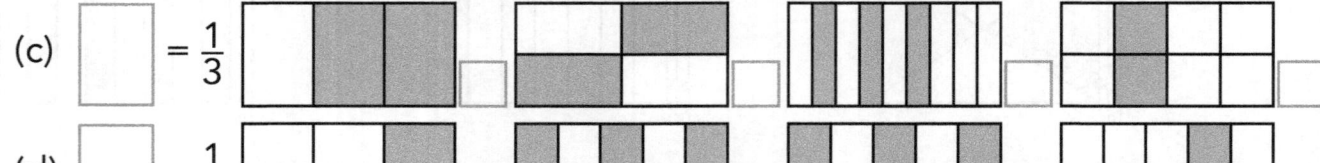

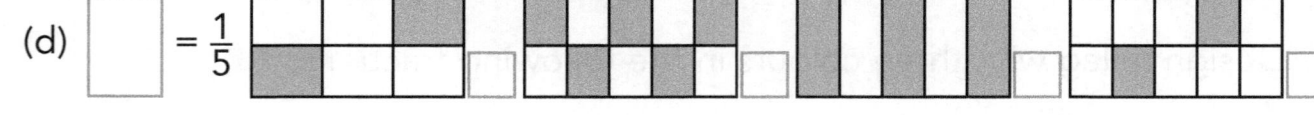

   (a) ☐ = $\frac{1}{2}$

   (b) ☐ = $\frac{1}{4}$

   (c) ☐ = $\frac{1}{3}$

   (d) ☐ = $\frac{1}{5}$

2. Look at the fractions that are shaded. Write each fraction in two ways.

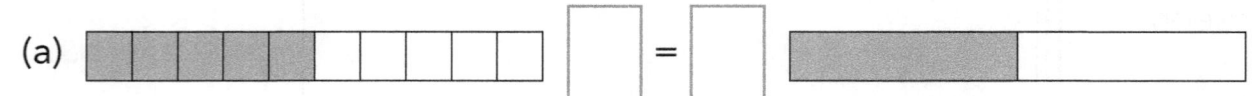

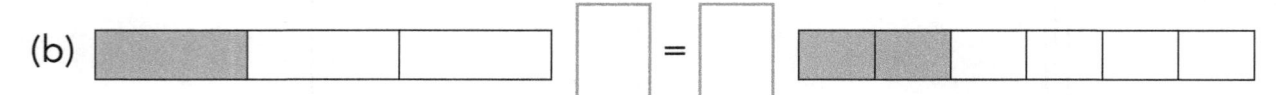

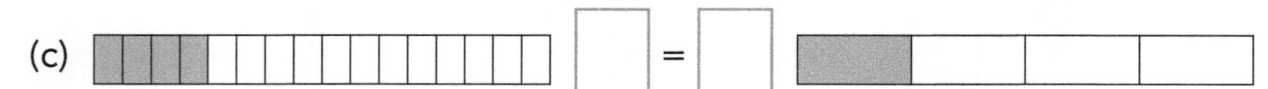

   (a) ☐ = ☐

   (b) ☐ = ☐

   (c) ☐ = ☐

   (d) ☐ = ☐

3. Circle the fraction in each set that is not equivalent.

   (a) $\frac{3}{4}$   $\frac{3}{12}$   $\frac{4}{16}$   $\frac{1}{4}$

   (b) $\frac{2}{12}$   $\frac{1}{2}$   $\frac{12}{24}$   $\frac{6}{12}$

   (c) $\frac{5}{15}$   $\frac{3}{30}$   $\frac{1}{3}$   $\frac{3}{9}$

## Fair fractions

Cutting food such as apples, oranges, cakes and bars of chocolate provides good opportunities to look at equivalent fractions. Cut an apple once and show two equal pieces or halves, then cut these halves to make quarters. Ask your child if they would prefer half an apple or two quarters. Show that two quarters is the same or equivalent to one half. Circular cakes are good to show thirds and sixths. Cut the cake into six equal parts and ask: How many sixths is the same a half of the cake? Ask your child if they would prefer a third of the cake or two-sixths. Group the pieces of cake into three equal parts to show that a third is the same as two-sixths.

# 8.4 Addition and subtraction of simple fractions

## Add and subtract fractions with the same denominator

1. Add these fractions.

   (a) $\frac{2}{7} + \frac{3}{7} = \square$

   (b) $\frac{4}{9} + \frac{4}{9} = \square$

   (c) $\frac{2}{8} + \frac{5}{8} = \square$

   (d) $\frac{5}{10} + \frac{3}{10} = \square$

   (e) $\frac{4}{7} + \frac{2}{7} = \square$

2. Subtract these fractions.

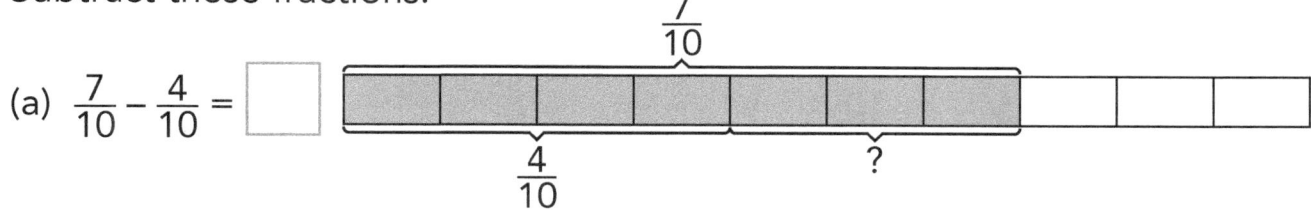

   (a) $\frac{7}{10} - \frac{4}{10} = \square$

   (b) $\frac{5}{9} - \frac{3}{9} = \square$

   (c) $\frac{4}{5} - \frac{3}{5} = \square$

   (d) $\frac{6}{7} - \frac{2}{7} = \square$

   (e) $\frac{8}{9} - \frac{4}{9} = \square$

## Fraction calculations

The bar model is a very useful visual image to help show the addition and subtraction of fractions. Draw a rectangle bar and ask your child to divide it into five equal parts, or fifths.

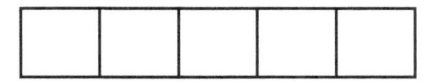

Ask your child to show you how they could label this bar model to demonstrate that $\frac{1}{5} + \frac{2}{5} = \frac{3}{5}$.

Repeat this for other fraction additions and subtractions. At this stage your child is only expected to add and subtract fractions with the same denominator (number below the line).

©HarperCollinsPublishers 2018

# 9.1 Multiplying by whole tens and hundreds (1)

## Multiply tens and hundreds by 1-digit numbers

1. Answer these.

   (a) 2 × 9 = ☐  (b) 7 × 4 = ☐  (c) 6 × 8 = ☐
   
   2 × 90 = ☐  7 × 40 = ☐  60 × 8 = ☐
   
   2 × 900 = ☐  700 × 4 = ☐  6 × 800 = ☐

2. Fill in the ◯ with >, < or = .

   (a) 3 × 50 ◯ 40 × 4    (b) 6 × 20 ◯ 30 × 4
   
   (c) 8 × 200 ◯ 800 × 2    (d) 700 × 3 ◯ 5 × 400
   
   (e) 5 × 500 ◯ 3 × 800    (f) 600 × 4 ◯ 8 × 30

3. Write the missing numbers.

   (a) ☐ × 4 = 1200    (b) 800 × ☐ = 1600
   
   (c) 2000 = ☐ × 5    (d) 2800 = 400 × ☐

4. Join multiplications with the same answer.

   80 × 3    10 × 8    40 × 2    60 × 8
   
   30 × 6                               50 × 3
   
   90 × 4                               30 × 5
   
   80 × 6    40 × 6    60 × 3    60 × 6

## Calculating coins

Place ten 20p coins in a pile. Ask your child to take part of the pile, count the coins and multiply by 20p to find the total value of the money they have in their hand, in pence. When they have tried this a few times, make it a little harder by taking away part of the pile and telling your child how many coins you have taken. Can they calculate how much is left in the pile, without counting the number of coins in the pile? Repeat this with a pile of ten 50p coins.

**You will need:** ten 20p coins, ten 50p coins.

# 9.2 Multiplying by whole tens and hundreds (2)

## Multiply tens and hundreds by 1-digit numbers

1. Calculate with reasoning.

   (a) 5 × 7 = ☐
   
   5 × 70 = ☐
   
   50 × 7 = ☐
   
   50 × 70 = ☐

   (b) 8 × 3 = ☐
   
   80 × 3 = ☐
   
   8 × 30 = ☐
   
   80 × 30 = ☐

   (c) 4 × 9 = ☐
   
   400 × 9 = ☐
   
   4 × 900 = ☐
   
   40 × 90 = ☐

2. Fill in the boxes.

   (a) 4 × 20 + 5 × 20
   
   = 9 × 20 = ☐

   (b) 2 × 300 + 6 × 300
   
   = 8 × 300 = ☐

   (c) 5 × 30 + 2 × 30
   
   = ☐ × 30 = ☐

   (d) 5 × 400 + 3 × 400
   
   = ☐ × ☐ = ☐

3. Answer these.

   (a) Sophie bought 9 boxes of pencils with 20 pencils in each. How many pencils did she buy?

   _____

   (b) Olivia drove 200 kilometres every day for 6 days. How far did she drive in total in the 6 days?

   _____

## 👪 Higher or lower?

Make a set of eight cards and write a number on each one: 200, 300, 400, 500, 600, 700, 800, 900. Shuffle the cards and lay them in a pile face down. Player 1 turns over the top card and says whether this card will be 'higher' or 'lower' than the target number of 2500 before rolling the dice. Player 1 rolls the dice and multiplies it by the card number. If the prediction is correct Player 1 keeps the card. Player 2 then takes a turn. The player with the most cards is the winner.

**You will need:** number cards, a dice.

# 9.3 Writing number sentences

## Write number sentences for multiplication problems

1. Write number sentences and then calculate.

   (a) There are 6 players in a hockey team. There are 11 teams in a hockey tournament. Each player pays £3 to enter the tournament. How much money does the tournament get in total?

   Number sentence: _____ Answer: ☐

   (b) A bottle of water costs £2 and there are 12 bottles in a pack. How much would it cost to buy 4 packs of water?

   Number sentence: _____ Answer: ☐

   (c) On a bus there are 4 seats in a row, a pair either side of the aisle. Each bus has 20 rows of seats. How many passengers will fit into 3 buses, if all the seats are full?

   Number sentence: _____ Answer: ☐

2. Look at the pictures. Write the number sentence and answer each question.

   Rice — 20kg £35    Apples — 12kg £20    Flour — 30kg £25

   (a) How much do 4 sacks of rice cost?

   Number sentence: _____ Answer: ☐

   (b) What is the weight of 7 boxes of apples?

   Number sentence: _____ Answer: ☐

   (c) I paid £50 for some flour. What is the total weight of the flour I bought?

   Number sentence: _____ Answer: ☐

## Number sentences

Use toys to make up and answer word problems, such as: These toy cars have four wheels. How many wheels would be on 60 cars? If there are 80 bricks in one box, how many would there be in seven similar boxes? This puzzle has 28 pieces. How many pieces in five similar puzzles? There are 64 crayons in a box. How many in three similar boxes?

# 9.4 Multiplying a 2-digit number by a 1-digit number (1)

## Multiply 2-digit numbers by 1-digit numbers

1. Complete these.

   (a) 31 × 5
   
   30 × 5 = ☐
   
   1 × 5 = ☐
   
   31 × 5 = ☐ + ☐ = ☐

   (b) 49 × 4
   
   40 × 4 = ☐
   
   9 × 4 = ☐
   
   49 × 4 = ☐ + ☐ = ☐

   (c) 26 × 8
   
   20 × 8 = ☐
   
   6 × 8 = ☐
   
   26 × 8 = ☐ + ☐ = ☐

   (d) 17 × 6
   
   10 × 6 = ☐
   
   7 × 6 = ☐
   
   17 × 6 = ☐ + ☐ = ☐

2. Answer these. Choose a method for working out each answer.

   (a) 86 × 2 = ☐
   
   (b) 3 × 47 = ☐
   
   (c) 19 × 9 = ☐
   
   (d) 8 × 23 = ☐

3. Read and answer these.

   (a) Mr Duke travels 19 km each day to and from work. He works 5 days a week. How far does he travel altogether in a week?

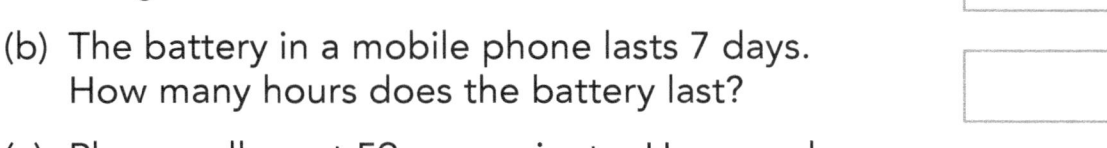

   (b) The battery in a mobile phone lasts 7 days. How many hours does the battery last?

   (c) Phone calls cost 59p per minute. How much will a 3-minute phone call cost?

## Ticket prices

Let your child help you work out everyday costs for the family. Look up the price of tickets: for theme parks, train journeys or the zoo. Check they are whole pound prices such as £24, not £24.50. Ask your child to calculate how much it will cost for a group of your family and friends (between 2 and 9 people) to visit these places.

# 9.5 Multiplying a 2-digit number by a 1-digit number (2)

## Multiply 2-digit numbers by 1-digit numbers

1. A drink costs 74p. How much do 3 drinks cost?

   $74 \times 3 = \boxed{\phantom{00}}$   Check the answer: $3 \times 74 = \boxed{\phantom{00}}$

   $$\begin{array}{r} 74 \\ \times \phantom{0}3 \\ \hline \phantom{00} \end{array}$$

   $3 \times 70 = \boxed{\phantom{00}}$

   $3 \times 4 = \boxed{\phantom{00}}$

   $\boxed{\phantom{00}} + \boxed{\phantom{00}} = \boxed{\phantom{00}}$

2. Use the column method to calculate. Remember to check your work.

   (a) $4 \times 72 = \boxed{\phantom{00}}$

   (b) $35 \times 3 = \boxed{\phantom{00}}$

   (c) $28 \times 5 = \boxed{\phantom{00}}$

   (d) $6 \times 43 = \boxed{\phantom{00}}$

3. Use the digits 4, 5 and 6.

   Arrange them to make different multiplications.  $\boxed{\phantom{0}}\boxed{\phantom{0}} \times \boxed{\phantom{0}} = ?$

   (a) What is the largest answer you can make? $\boxed{\phantom{00}}$

   (b) What is the smallest answer? $\boxed{\phantom{00}}$

   (c) What answer is the nearest to 300? $\boxed{\phantom{00}}$

## Column method

Ask your child to explain to you the column method they use to multiply numbers. Check that they understand that, for example, for 68 × 4, 68 is 60 + 8 so they multiply the tens and the ones by 4 and add the two products together. Try different examples so they are confident with this written method.

# 9.6 Multiplying a 2-digit number by a 1-digit number (3)

## Multiply 2-digit numbers by 1-digit numbers

| N | H | Z | I | A | M | G | T | S |
|---|---|---|---|---|---|---|---|---|
| 186 | 153 | 158 | 194 | 168 | 120 | 184 | 144 | 171 |

Multiply these and match each answer to a letter. Re-arrange the letters to find the secret message.

| 56 × 3 | 31 × 6 | 79 × 2 | 17 × 9 |
|---|---|---|---|
| Code letter ☐ | Code letter ☐ | Code letter ☐ | Code letter ☐ |

| 24 × 7 | 15 × 8 | 36 × 4 | 42 × 4 |
|---|---|---|---|
| Code letter ☐ | Code letter ☐ | Code letter ☐ | Code letter ☐ |

| 97 × 2 | 28 × 6 | 23 × 8 | 16 × 9 |
|---|---|---|---|
| Code letter ☐ | Code letter ☐ | Code letter ☐ | Code letter ☐ |

| 57 × 3 | 24 × 5 |
|---|---|
| Code letter ☐ | Code letter ☐ |

Secret message is: ☐☐☐☐☐☐☐ ☐☐ ☐☐☐☐☐

## Multiplication codes

Try making up your own multiplication codes to give messages to each other. Keep it simple to begin with, perhaps concentrating just on multiplication facts up to 12 × 12 as the numbers related to different letters. A way to approach it is to think of a message and then give the answer to a multiplication fact for each of the letters in the message. The letters can then be rearranged onto a grid so the message is presented as a code with multiplication facts for each letter.

(Answer: AMAZING AT MATHS)

# 9.7 Multiplying a 3-digit number by a 1-digit number (1)

## Multiply 3-digit numbers by 1-digit numbers

1. Complete these.

   (a) 421 × 5

   400 × 5 = ☐

   20 × 5 = ☐

   1 × 5 = ☐

   421 × 5 = ☐ + ☐ + ☐

   (b) 346 × 2

   300 × 2 = ☐

   40 × 2 = ☐

   6 × 2 = ☐

   346 × 2 = ☐ + ☐ + ☐

   (c) 538 × 3

   500 × 3 = ☐

   30 × 3 = ☐

   8 × 3 = ☐

   538 × 3 = ☐ + ☐ + ☐

   (d) 275 × 4

   200 × 4 = ☐

   70 × 4 = ☐

   5 × 4 = ☐

   275 × 4 = ☐ + ☐ + ☐

2. Answer these. Choose a method for working out each answer.

   (a) 354 × 7 = ☐

   (b) 4 × 291 = ☐

   (c) 604 × 9 = ☐

   (d) 6 × 485 = ☐

3. Read and answer these.
   (a) A train carriage holds 128 passengers. How many people will a train with 6 carriages hold?
   (b) There are 240 teabags in a large box. How many teabags are there in 4 boxes?
   (c) A fence is built with 5 wooden panels each 180 cm wide. What is the length of the fence in total?

## 👪 Multiplication

When shopping or in your kitchen cupboards, look for multipacks, such as four 415 g cans of beans, and ask: How much does each multipack weigh? You can ask in the style of a maths question to help your child develop understanding of word problems, for example: There are four cans of beans each weighing 415 g. What is the total weight of this multipack?

# 9.8 Multiplying a 3-digit number by a 1-digit number (2)

## Multiply 3-digit numbers by 1-digit numbers

1. Answer these.

   (a) Estimate: 200 × 2 = ☐

   ```
       2  2  4
   ×         2
   ─────────────
   ```

   (b) Estimate: 150 × 3 = ☐

   ```
       1  5  3
   ×         3
   ─────────────
   ```

   (c) Estimate: 600 × 4 = ☐

   ```
       6  3  1
   ×         4
   ─────────────
   ```

   (d) Estimate: 200 × 8 = ☐

   ```
       1  9  5
   ×         8
   ─────────────
   ```

2. Work out the total weight for each of these.

   (a) Rice 750 g, Rice 750 g, Rice 750 g ☐

   (b) Salt 380 g, Salt 380 g, Salt 380 g, Salt 380 g ☐

   (c) Coffee 295 g, Coffee 295 g, Coffee 295 g, Coffee 295 g ☐

   (d) Jam 245 g, Jam 245 g, Jam 245 g, Jam 245 g ☐

## Multiplication challenge

**You will need:** paper, dice.

Draw two 3 by 3 grids, one for you and one for your child. Each of you should write the digits 1–9 in the squares in any order. Look at the 3-digit numbers in each column and row. Talk about which are the smallest and largest 3-digit numbers. Both of you roll a dice and then choose which column or row you will multiply by that number. You can complete your calculations at the same time.

The overall aim of the game is to be the player with the smallest and the largest product. So if either of you roll a low number it would be best to multiply it by your smallest number and, if you roll a high number, you should multiply it by your largest number. Roll the dice six times so you have a product for each column and row on your grid. It is good to play this a second time, to give you the opportunity to refine your strategy.

©HarperCollinsPublishers 2018

# 9.9 Practice and exercise

## Solve multiplication problems

1. Fill in the ◯ with >, < or = .

   (a)  49 × 3 ◯ 153      (b)  204 ◯ 52 × 0      (c)  27 × 6 ◯ 26 × 7

   (d)  185 × 4 ◯ 460     (e)  390 × 2 ◯ 778 + 2    (f)  1600 ◯ 540 × 3

2. Write the number sentences and then calculate.

   (a) What is the product of 380 and 4?  _____

   (b) What is the product of 540 and 6?  _____

   (c) What is 5 times two hundred and thirty-six? _____

   (d) What is 816 multiplied by 3?  _____

3. Look at the masses of these large animals.

   African elephant 4800 kg    White rhino 2200 kg    Zebra 285 kg    Giraffe 800 kg    Polar bear 475 kg

   (a) Will 6 giraffes weight more, less or the same as 1 elephant?  _____

   (b) Will 5 polar bears weigh more, less or the same as 1 rhino?  _____

   (c) Will 3 giraffes weigh more, less or the same as 9 zebras?  _____

   (d) Will 5 zebras weigh more, less or the same as 3 polar bears?  _____

## Holiday costs

Look at prices of holidays under £1000 per person and calculate how much it would cost your family or a group of friends to go on holiday. Children enjoy role play and they could be the travel agent. Start with using the same price per person for everyone, then they could calculate different costs for adults and children. For example: The cost of a one-week family holiday is £475 per person. How much will it cost a family of four to go on this holiday? The cost of a holiday is £328 per adult and £247 for children. How much would this cost a family of two adults and four children?

# 9.10 Dividing whole tens and whole hundreds

## Use division facts to divide multiples of 10 and 100

1. Work out the missing numbers.

   (a) ☐ × 30 = 240   (b) ☐ × 50 = 450   (c) 60 × ☐ = 420

   240 ÷ 30 = ☐     450 ÷ 50 = ☐      420 ÷ 60 = ☐

   240 ÷ ☐ = 30     450 ÷ ☐ = 50      420 ÷ ☐ = 60

2. Answer these.

   (a) 140 ÷ 2 = ☐    (b) 300 ÷ 5 = ☐    (c) 240 ÷ 8 = ☐

   140 ÷ 20 = ☐      300 ÷ 50 = ☐       240 ÷ 80 = ☐

   (d) 360 ÷ 4 = ☐    (e) 270 ÷ 3 = ☐    (f) 450 ÷ 9 = ☐

   360 ÷ 40 = ☐      270 ÷ 30 = ☐       450 ÷ 90 = ☐

3. Solve these problems.

   (a) A garden path is made by laying square paving tiles side by side. The path is 210 cm long and the tiles are 30 cm wide and 30 cm long. How many tiles are needed for this path?

   (b) I have read 4 times the number of pages as I still have left to read in my book. The book has a total of 450 pages. How many pages do I still have to left to read?

   (c) At a school a race track is 80 m long. How many laps must be completed for a 400 m race?

## Division

Ask your child to look for patterns in the answers for Question 2. They should understand why the answer to the second part of each pair of questions is 10 times smaller as it is being divided by a number that is 10 times larger. It will show their understanding of place value. Give an example such as:

15 ÷ 3 =

150 ÷ 30 =

Talk about the reasons why these have the same answer.

©HarperCollinsPublishers 2018

# 9.11 Dividing a 2-digit number by a 1-digit number (1)

## Divide 2-digit numbers by 1-digit numbers

1. Complete these multiplication and division facts.

    (a) 9  4  36     9 × ☐ = ☐     ☐ ÷ 9 = ☐
                     4 × ☐ = ☐     ☐ ÷ 4 = ☐

    (b) 45  5  9     ☐ × ☐ = ☐     ☐ ÷ ☐ = ☐
                     ☐ × ☐ = ☐     ☐ ÷ ☐ = ☐

    (c) 6  42  7     ☐ × ☐ = ☐     ☐ ÷ ☐ = ☐
                     ☐ × ☐ = ☐     ☐ ÷ ☐ = ☐

    (d) 56  7  8     ☐ × ☐ = ☐     ☐ ÷ ☐ = ☐
                     ☐ × ☐ = ☐     ☐ ÷ ☐ = ☐

2. Find the greatest number that will fill in each box.

    (a) 4 × ☐ < 30      (b) ☐ × 6 < 35      (c) ☐ × 5 < 47
    (d) 8 × ☐ < 60      (e) 3 × ☐ < 23      (f) ☐ × 9 < 85

3. Answer these.

    (a) 65 ÷ 5           (b) 56 ÷ 4           (c) 98 ÷ 7
        30 ÷ 5 = ☐           16 ÷ 4 = ☐           28 ÷ 7 = ☐
        35 ÷ 5 = ☐           40 ÷ 4 = ☐           70 ÷ 7 = ☐
        65 ÷ 5 = ☐           56 ÷ 4 = ☐           98 ÷ 7 = ☐

## Dividing with counters

**You will need:** counters.

Using counters, buttons or building bricks, ask your child to show different multiplications by laying the counters in rows and columns on a piece of paper. Ask your child to write the answer and then check by counting the counters. They may count in steps, so, for example, if it is 6 × 7 they can count in steps of 6s or 7s. Now ask your child to write the matching pairs of division 42 ÷ 6 and 42 ÷ 7, pointing to the rows or columns to find the answers. It is important that children recognise the relationship between multiplication and division.

# 9.12 Dividing a 2-digit number by a 1-digit number (2)

**Divide 2-digit numbers by 1-digit numbers**

1. Use the column method to calculate these.

   (a) 3 ) 4 8     (b) 5 ) 7 5     (c) 4 ) 6 8     (d) 8 ) 8 8

2. Use the column method to calculate these.

   (a) 58 ÷ 2 = ☐     (b) 85 ÷ 5 = ☐     (c) 68 ÷ 4 = ☐

3. Answer these division problems.

   (a) There are 84 children in Year 3 and they are divided into three equal sized classes. How many children are there in each class?

   _____

   (b) A baker makes 90 bread rolls and sells them in packs of 6. How many packs of rolls will there be?

   _____

   (c) Lee plants a sunflower seed and it takes 98 days for it to grow and the flower to open. How many weeks does it take?

   _____

## Division

Check that your child understands the column method of division when dividing a 2-digit number by a 1-digit number. Remind them that the first digit in the 2-digit number is a tens number and ask them to tell you about the relationship between, for example, 8 ÷ 4 and 80 ÷ 4. It is important for children to line up the columns in the division accurately and record numbers left over so that they are not forgotten in the final calculation.

# 9.13 Dividing a 2-digit number by a 1-digit number (3)

## Divide 2-digit numbers by 1-digit numbers

1. Use the column method to calculate these with remainders.

   (a) 3 ) 4 9   (b) 4 ) 7 9   (c) 5 ) 6 8   (d) 3 ) 8 6

2. Use the column method to calculate these with remainders.

   (a) 47 ÷ 2 = ☐   (b) 93 ÷ 5 = ☐   (c) 81 ÷ 4 = ☐

3. A group of 65 school children go to a theme park and all of the children go on each ride. The rides have different numbers of seats and carriages. Read and answer these.

   (a) The Roller Coaster has 3 seats in a row. How many full rows will there be? How many children will be in the last row?

   _____

   (b) The boats on the River Ride each hold 7 children. The boats have to be full, so teachers fill the empty seats in the last boat. How many teachers will there be in the last boat?

   _____

## 👪 Mini world division

Use farm toys, cars, trucks and other small world toys you have to make division problems. Build fields and say that a farmer wants the same number of animals in each field. How many will be in each field and how many will be left over? Change the number of fields. In the same way ask for the same number of cars to be parked in a given number of rows. How many cars are left over?

**You will need:** small world toys.

# 9.14 Dividing a 2-digit number by a 1-digit number (4)

## Divide 2-digit numbers by 1-digit numbers

1. Answer these. What do you notice?

    (a) 54 ÷ 3 = ☐      (b) 84 ÷ 3 = ☐      (c) 68 ÷ 2 = ☐      (d) 96 ÷ 4 = ☐

    54 ÷ 6 = ☐          84 ÷ 6 = ☐          68 ÷ 4 = ☐          96 ÷ 8 = ☐

2. Fill in the boxes.

    (a) 48 ÷ [4 / 6 / 8] = ☐

    (b) 60 ÷ [3 / 4 / 5] = ☐

    (c) 36 ÷ [3 / 6 / 9] = ☐

    (d) 72 ÷ [4 / 6 / 8] = ☐

3. Sam plants some lettuces in his garden.

    He estimated that he had between 30 and 50 lettuces on his plot.
    He counted them in fours. There were 2 left over.
    He counted them in fives. There was 1 left over.

    How many lettuces did Sam have? ☐

---

### Estimate how many

**You will need:** counters or other small objects.

Using counters, buttons, building bricks or any small objects, take a handful and place them in a pile. Without counting, ask your child to estimate how many there are. Both of you take away groups of five as fast as you can. How many are left over?

Without counting the total, place the objects back in a middle pile and take away groups of eight. How many are left over? Together, work out the possible number of objects.

When you have a few possible numbers, look at the pile and decide which number it might be. Count the objects to check your answer. Repeat with different handfuls and counting them in different groups, such as groups of nine and seven or any other pairs of numbers.

©HarperCollinsPublishers 2018

# 9.15 Dividing a 2-digit number by a 1-digit number (5)

## Divide 2-digit numbers by 1-digit numbers

1. Use the column method to calculate. Check your answers.
   (a) 75 ÷ 4 =
   (b) 75 ÷ 6 =
   (c) 75 ÷ 8 =

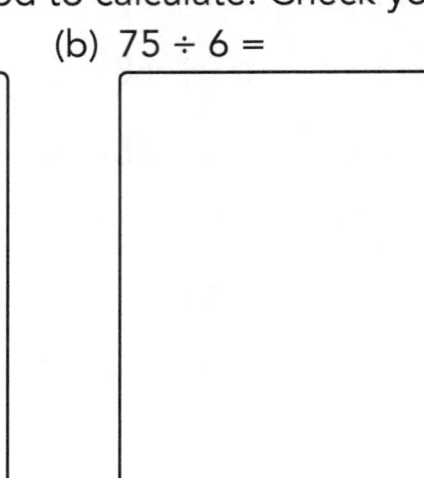

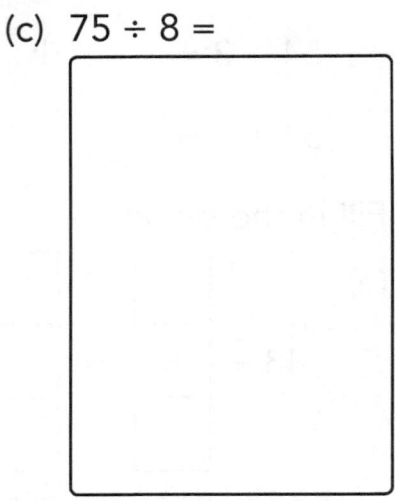

2. Join each division to the correct remainder.

   | 38 ÷ 5 | r 1 | 19 ÷ 3 |
   | 40 ÷ 6 | r 2 | 27 ÷ 4 |
   | 74 ÷ 8 | r 3 | 82 ÷ 9 |
   | 23 ÷ 7 | r 4 | 44 ÷ 8 |

3. In a box of beads there are 3 times as many white beads as blue beads. There are 58 blue beads. Answer these.
   (a) How many beads are there in total?
   (b) Necklaces are made using 9 white beads each. How many necklaces can be made?
   (c) Equal number of blue beads are added to each of these white necklaces. How many blue beads will there be left over?

## Division

**You will need:** a dice.

Make a large 10 by 6 grid on a piece of paper. Write in each number from 1 to 60, starting at the top left corner. Roll a dice and start on that number, dividing every number by the number rolled and writing a division and a remainder. If you roll a 4, start on 4 and write 4 ÷ 4 = 1, then go on to 5 ÷ 4 = 1 r 1, 6 ÷ 4 = 1 r 2 and so on until you get to 60. This can be repeated using different divisors.

# 9.16 Dividing a 3-digit number by a 1-digit number (1)

## Divide 3-digit numbers by 1-digit numbers

1. Write the answers, with remainders if needed. Start with the tables and then return to the question to add part quotients together.

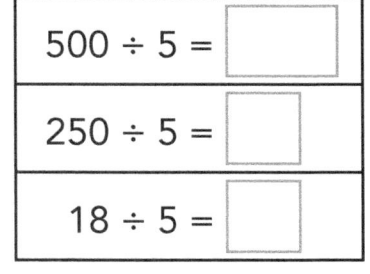

    (a) $485 \div 4 =$ ☐   (b) $729 \div 3 =$ ☐   (c) $768 \div 5 =$ ☐

    | $400 \div 4 =$ | $600 \div 3 =$ | $500 \div 5 =$ |
    | $80 \div 4 =$  | $120 \div 3 =$ | $250 \div 5 =$ |
    | $5 \div 4 =$   | $9 \div 3 =$   | $18 \div 5 =$  |

2. Set out each calculation using the column representation.

    (a) 4 ) 4 8 5

    (b) 3 ) 7 2 9

    (c) 6 ) 7 5 8

3. Look at these numbers.

    736   924   310   496   612   548

    (a) Which of these numbers can be divided exactly by 4? _____

    (b) Which of these numbers can be divided exactly by 8? _____

## 👪 Division

In Question 1 the column method for dividing is broken down into parts so children can see the whole numbers that are being divided in this process. If you look at Question 2, in the column method adults tend to say 4 can be divided into 4 one time, whereas what is actually happening is 400 is being divided by 4 one hundred times. In the second example 7 (700) divided by 3, is shown as $600 \div 3 = 200$, with the 100 carried into $120 \div 3$.

©HarperCollinsPublishers 2018

# 9.17 Dividing a 3-digit number by a 1-digit number (2)

## Divide 3-digit numbers by 1-digit numbers

1. Choose from these numbers to answer each question.

   | 173 | 195 | 184 | 186 | 181 |

   (a) Which two of these numbers leave a remainder of 1 when divided by 5?
   _____

   (b) Which number divides exactly by 6?
   _____

   (c) Which number leaves a remainder of 3 when divided by 4?
   _____

   (d) Which number leaves a remainder of 1 when divided by 9?
   _____

2. Find three numbers between 100 and 140 that have:
   - a remainder of 1 when divided by 2
   - a remainder of 3 when divided by 4
   - a remainder of 5 when divided by 6.

   _____

   Can you predict the next two numbers after 140 that will have the same remainders? ☐ ☐

   Check your prediction by dividing.

## What is my number?

Make questions like these for your child:

The number I am thinking of has a remainder of 2 when divided by 3 and is an even number between 20 and 29. What is my number?

The number I am thinking of has a remainder of 5 when divided by 7 and is between 40 and 49.

Use small numbers up to 50 until your child is confident and then continue with numbers up to 150.

# 9.18 Dividing a 3-digit number by a 1-digit number (3)

## Divide 3-digit numbers by 1-digit numbers

1. Answer these.

    (a) 447 ÷ 4 = ☐
    (b) 619 ÷ 3 = ☐
    (c) 837 ÷ 5 = ☐
    (d) 703 ÷ 8 = ☐

2. Work out the missing numbers.

    (a) ☐ × 4 = 548
    (b) 9 × ☐ = 387
    (c) ☐ ÷ 6 = 450
    (d) 615 ÷ ☐ = 5

3. Complete these division towers.

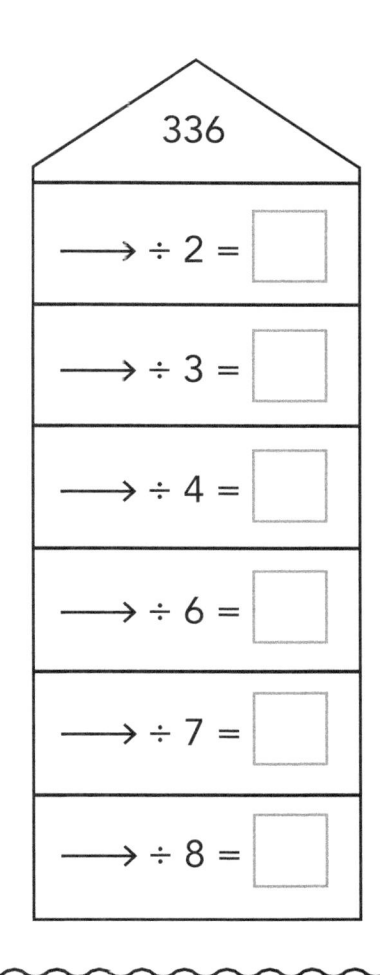

    Tower 1: 720
    ⟶ ÷ 3 = ☐
    ⟶ ÷ 4 = ☐
    ⟶ ÷ 5 = ☐
    ⟶ ÷ 6 = ☐
    ⟶ ÷ 8 = ☐
    ⟶ ÷ 9 = ☐

    Tower 2: 336
    ⟶ ÷ 2 = ☐
    ⟶ ÷ 3 = ☐
    ⟶ ÷ 4 = ☐
    ⟶ ÷ 6 = ☐
    ⟶ ÷ 7 = ☐
    ⟶ ÷ 8 = ☐

## Division puzzles

Say to your child: I'm thinking of a number between 400 and 500. When it is divided by 2, 3 or 5 it does not leave a remainder. Which three numbers could I be thinking of? (Answers: 420, 450, 480)

Ask your child to make up their own puzzles like this.

©HarperCollinsPublishers 2018

# 9.19 Application of division

## Use division to solve practical problems

1. Read and answer these.

   (a) There are 365 days in a common year. How many full weeks are in a year and how many days are left over?

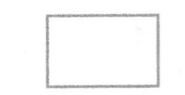

   (b) A floor is 496 cm long and floor tiles are 8 cm in length. How many tiles will be needed to cover one whole length of the floor?

   (c) A car park holds 756 cars equally on 9 levels. How many cars can be parked on each level?

   (d) A reel of electric cable is 500 m in length. It is cut into 7 m lengths. How many 7 m lengths will there be and how much is left over?

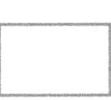

2. Matt has a collection of badges that he wants to count. He knows that he has between 120 and 150 badges, but not the exact number. He decides to count them in fives, and he has 2 left over. He then counts them in sixes and he has 3 left over.

   Can you work out exactly how many badges Matt has?

### Division challenge

**You will need:** paper, pencils.

Help your child visualise a word problem by using drawings and practical resources. Talk through the problem and different ways to represent the calculation.

Challenge: A picture frame measures 270 cm around its outside edge. The width of the frame is double the length of the height of the frame.

What is the difference in size between the height of the sides and the width of the frame? Make the frame using pencils and ask: If one pencil represents the height, how many pencils are needed for the width? How many pencils in total are needed around the whole picture? This should help them to realise they need to divide the whole length by six.

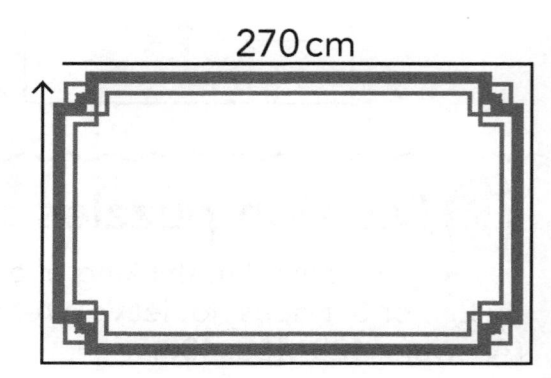

# 9.20 Finding the total price

**Use division to solve practical problems**

1. Fill in the table.

| Type of tyre | Bicycle tyre | Car tyre | Lorry tyre |
|---|---|---|---|
| Price per wheel | £35 | £50 | £ |
| Number of wheels | 2 | | 6 |
| Total price | £ | £200 | £420 |

2. Use the chart and fill in the ◯ with × or ÷.

   (a) Price per wheel ◯ Number of wheels = Total price

   (b) Total price ◯ Price per wheel = Number of wheels

   (c) Total price ◯ Number of wheels = Price per wheel

3. Answer these.

   (a) A farmer has 12 chickens and each chicken lays an egg every day. How many egg cartons, which hold 6 eggs each, can be filled in one week?

   (b) A hockey team spends £720 on 100 hockey sticks. There are 5 sticks in a box. How much do 2 boxes of hockey sticks cost?

   (c) A school is painted over the summer holiday and 456 litres of paint is used. The paint is in pots of 8 litres and costs £5 a pot. How much is spent on paint in total?

   (d) In a school there are 6 times as many children as adults. There are 510 children. How many adults and children are there in total?

## Division

Give your child the digits 1, 2 and 6 and ask them to make as many 3-digit numbers as they can. Write them in size order, starting with the smallest, as headings, each with a column below. Divide each number by all the numbers between two and nine, writing the answers with remainders if needed. What do they notice about their answers? Which numbers were not divisible by two? Which numbers divided exactly into all the 3-digit numbers? What do they notice about the remainders? Repeat with any other three digits.

©HarperCollinsPublishers 2018

# 10.1 Angles

## Identify and explore angles

1. Look at these shapes.

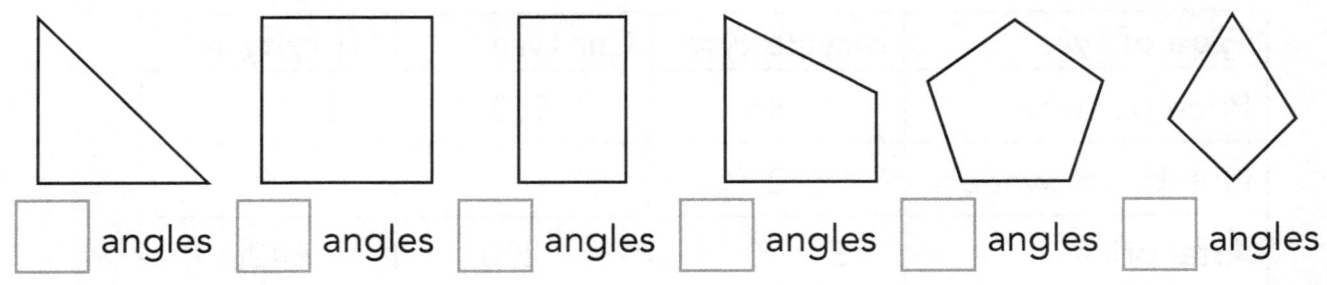

   ☐ angles   ☐ angles   ☐ angles   ☐ angles   ☐ angles   ☐ angles

   (a) Write the number of angles there are in each shape.

   (b) Draw a dot in each right angle on these shapes.

2. These angles have been made by joining three dots.

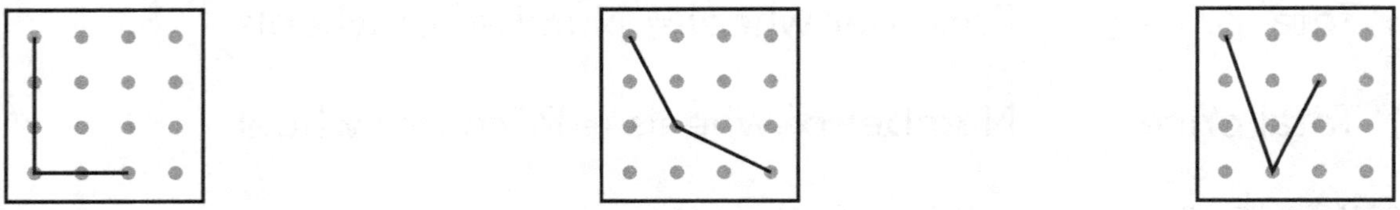

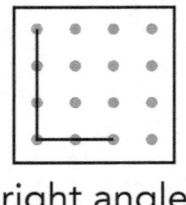

   right angle         obtuse angle         acute angle

   Join three dots on these grids. Make different angles of each type.

   (a) Right angles

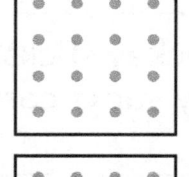

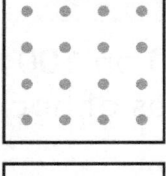

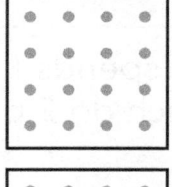

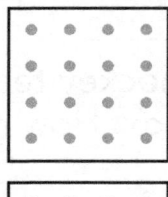

   (b) Obtuse angles

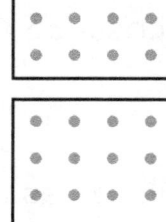

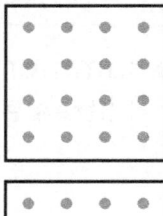

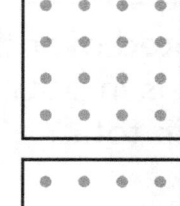

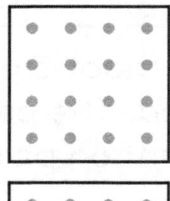

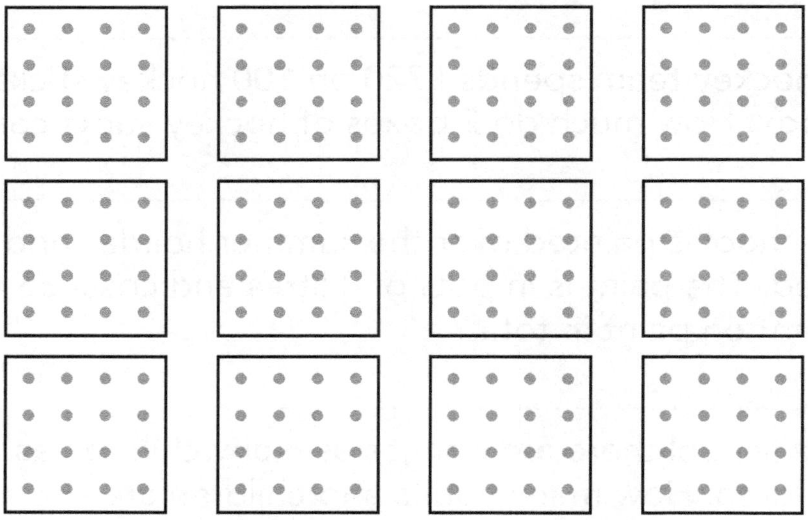

   (c) Acute angles

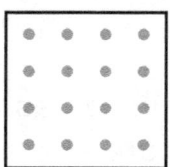

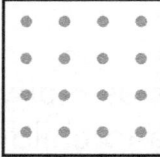

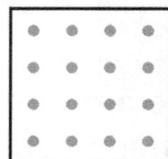

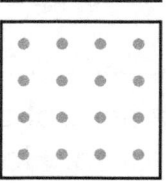

## Right angles

Ask your child to make a right-angle measurer by folding over a piece of paper once and then a second time so that the crease is folded exactly on top of itself.

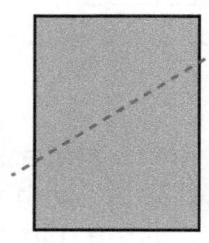

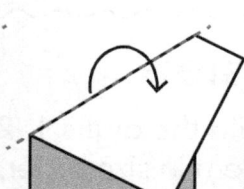

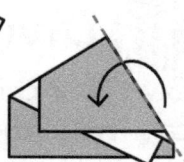

Use the right-angle measurer to find right angles around the house, putting the paper corner inside the angle to check. Use the words 'acute' for angles less than a right angle and 'obtuse' for angles greater than a right angle.

# 10.2 Identifying different types of line (1)

## Identify horizontal and vertical lines

1. Tick the horizontal lines.

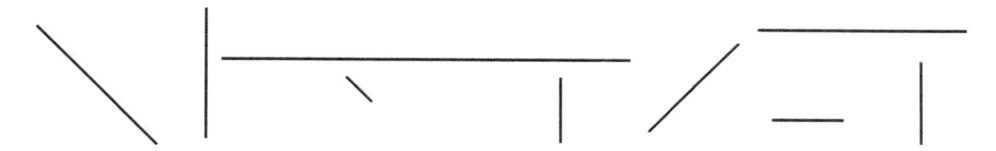

2. Draw a red line over the vertical fence posts.

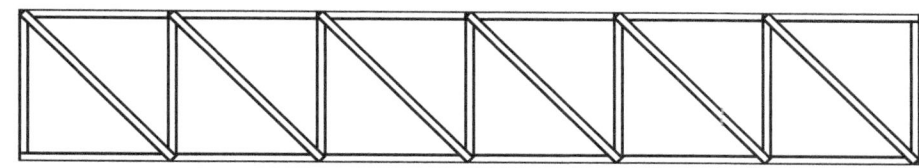

3. Write the words in the correct positions.

   | Complete turn    Quarter turn    Half turn    Three-quarter turn |
   |---|

   (a)

   (b)

   _____

   (c)

   (d)

   _____

4. True or false? (Put a ✓ for true and a ✗ for false in each box.)
   (a) After a half turn, a vertical line is still a vertical line. ☐
   (b) After a quarter turn, a vertical line is still a vertical line. ☐
   (c) After a three-quarter turn, a vertical line will become a horizontal line. ☐
   (d) After a complete turn, a horizontal line is still a horizontal line. ☐

## 👪 Lines

Look around your house for vertical and horizontal lines. Which sides of a door or window are horizontal and which are vertical? Look at patterns on wallpaper, curtains, clothes and packaging and identify vertical and horizontal lines.

# 10.3 Identifying different types of line (2)

## Identify perpendicular and parallel lines

1. Tick any of these that are vertical, or perpendicular, to the ground.

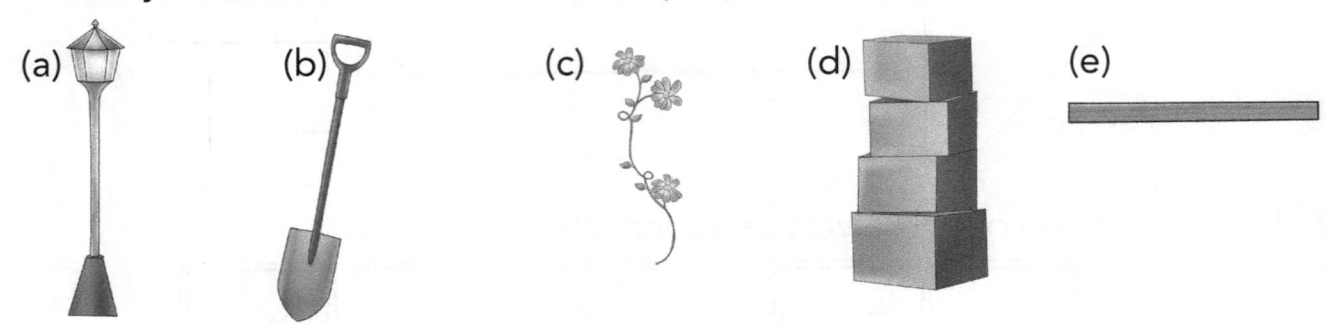

   (a)     (b)     (c)     (d)     (e)

2. Draw over pairs of parallel lines on these shapes. Use pairs of matching colours to show them.

3. Use a ruler to draw a horizontal straight line in this box.

   Draw three lines that are perpendicular to your horizontal line. Make each line a different length.

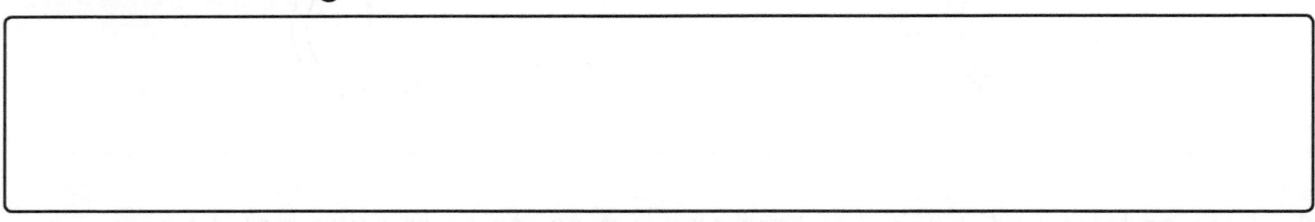

   Are the three lines you have drawn parallel to each other?   Yes / No

4. Which of these capital letters has three parallel lines and a line perpendicular to them? Circle your answer.

   E     F     H     I     L

## Parallel lines

Look for parallel lines around you. Look at bricks on walls, paving slabs, fence panels, double yellow lines on the road, painted lines on sports courts, and identify the pairs of parallel lines. Parallel lines are not always horizontal or vertical; look for parallel lines on road signs and other diagonal parallel lines.

# 10.4 Drawing 2-D shapes and making 3-D shapes

## Explore properties of 2-D and 3-D shapes

1. These are sketches of shapes so the lengths are not accurate.

    Use a ruler and pencil to draw each shape accurately.

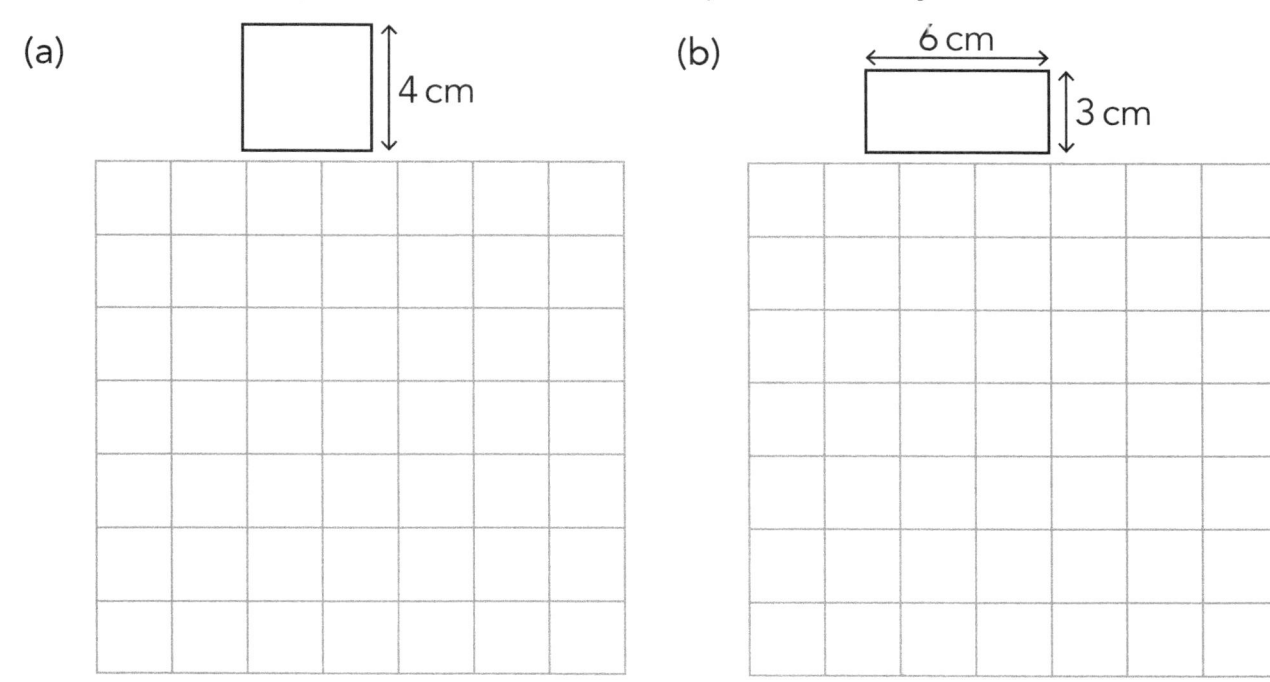

    (a) 4 cm

    (b) 6 cm, 3 cm

2. Draw a cuboid or cube using this method.

    **1** Draw a rectangle   **2** Draw another rectangle   **3** Join the corners

    Try drawing different types of cuboids in this way.

## Drawing shapes

Encourage your child to draw and paint pictures that have shapes in them and talk about the shapes. Draw a building with a roof, windows and doors. What shapes have you drawn? Draw a lorry and cars with windows, doors and wheels. Can you see any shapes you have drawn? Help your child to draw a 3-D house, using the method in Question 2. Draw the lines in pencil and then look at a real house and consider which sides you can see at the same time; draw darker lines to show the front and one side.

# 10.5 Length: metre, centimetre and millimetre

## Measure and compare lengths using metres, centimetres and millimetres

1. Measure each pencil and write its length.

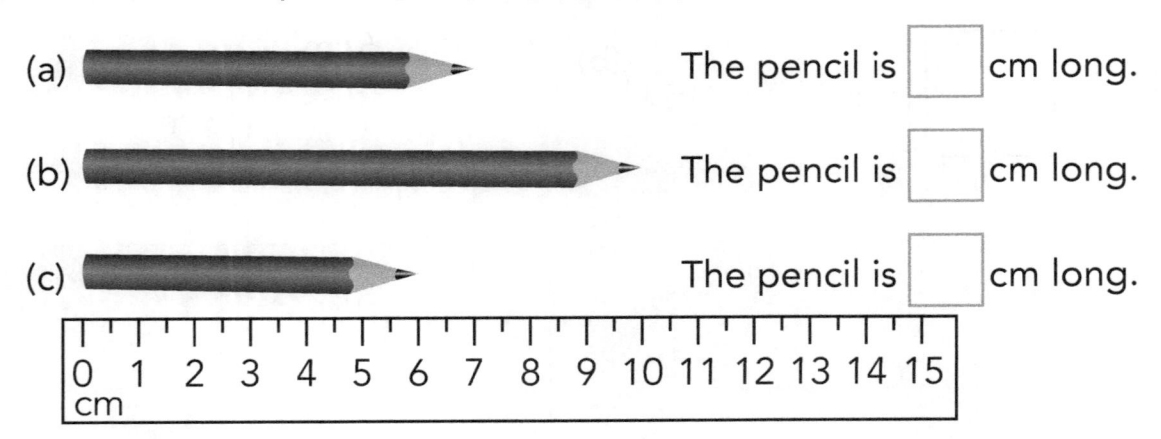

   (a) The pencil is ☐ cm long.

   (b) The pencil is ☐ cm long.

   (c) The pencil is ☐ cm long.

2. Write <, > or = to make each sentence true.

   > Remember: < means 'is less than'
   > > means 'is greater than'

   (a) 1 m 86 cm ◯ 168 cm
   (b) 1 m 10 cm ◯ 110 mm
   (c) 472 cm ◯ 4 m 72 cm
   (d) 9 cm ◯ 900 mm
   (e) 835 cm ◯ 8 m 35 cm
   (f) 106 mm ◯ 160 cm

3. Would you use metres or centimetres to measure these distances? Write centimetres or metres for each of these.

   (a) the width of a book        _____

   (b) the distance around your waist   _____

   (c) the length of your bedroom     _____

   (d) the length of a football pitch    _____

## Measuring

**You will need:** a 30 cm ruler.

Use a 30 cm ruler to measure objects around the house, such as spoons, pencils, screwdriver, screws, paperclips and pegs. Ask your child to draw a line for each one, using the ruler so that it is the same length as the real object. Lay the object on top of the drawing to check the accuracy of the measuring.

# 10.6 Perimeters of simple 2-D shapes (1)

## Calculate and measure the perimeters of simple 2-D shapes

1. Work out the perimeter of each of these shapes.

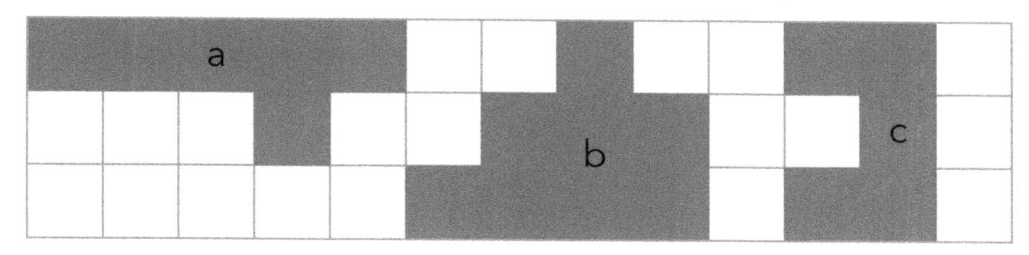

   (a) Perimeter = ☐ cm   (b) Perimeter = ☐ cm   (c) Perimeter = ☐ cm

2. On this grid, draw a shape with a perimeter of 16 cm.

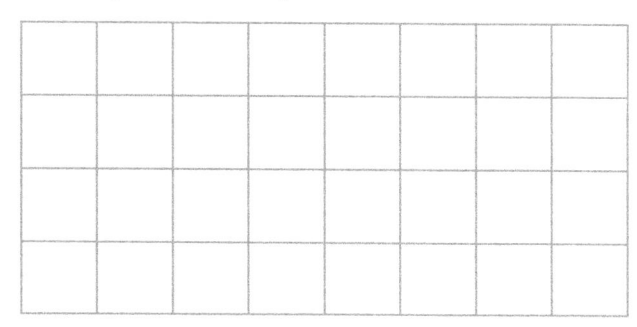

3. Calculate the perimeter of each of these shapes (drawings not to scale).

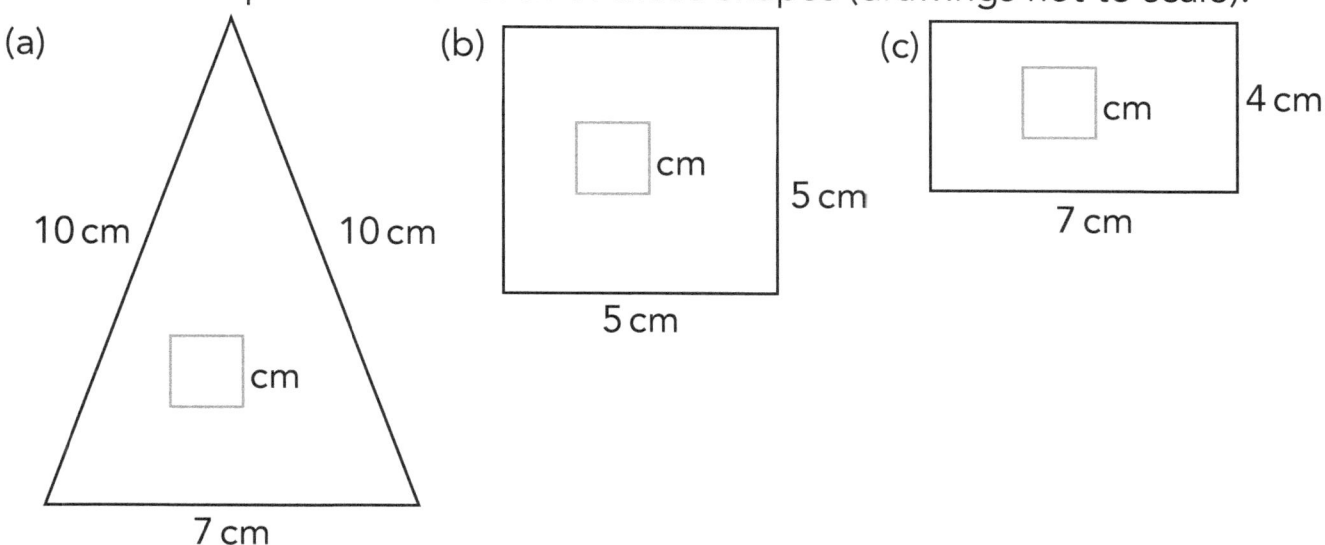

   (a) Triangle: 10 cm, 10 cm, 7 cm — Perimeter = ☐ cm

   (b) Square: 5 cm, 5 cm — Perimeter = ☐ cm

   (c) Rectangle: 7 cm, 4 cm — Perimeter = ☐ cm

## Perimeter

Use building bricks that are all the same size and make different size pens and fields for animals in a farmyard. Count the outside face of the bricks to find the perimeter of each field.

**You will need:** building bricks of the same size.

# 10.7 Perimeters of simple 2-D shapes (2)

## Calculate and measure the perimeters of simple 2-D shapes

1. Calculate the distance round each of these. Write the perimeters in cm.

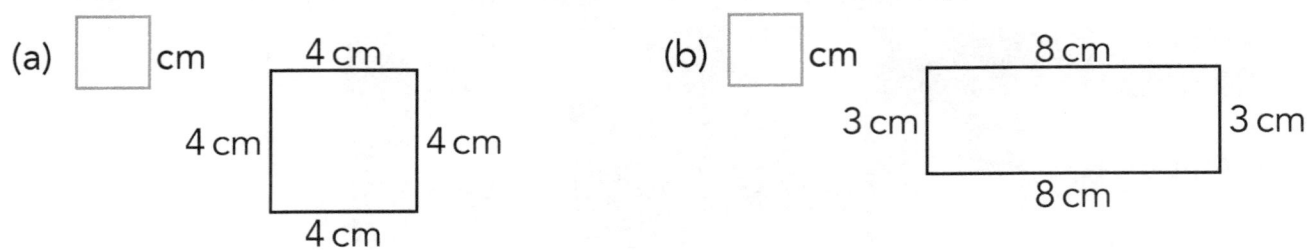

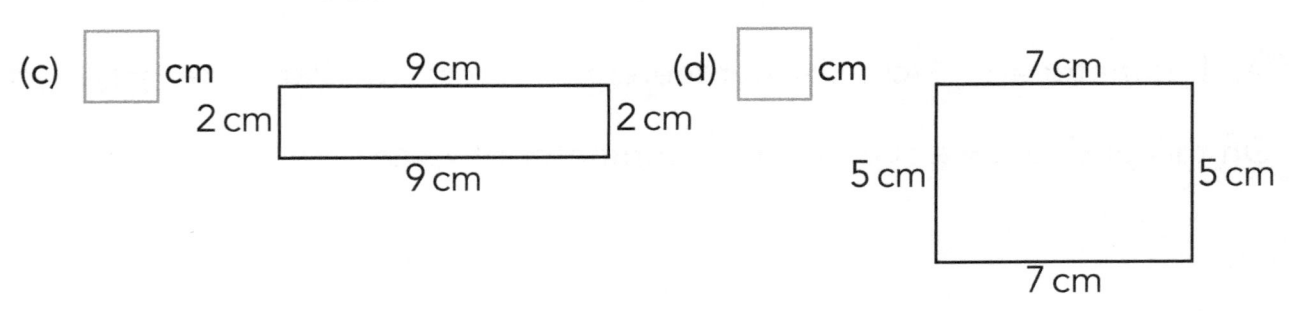

   (a) ☐ cm   4 cm / 4 cm / 4 cm / 4 cm

   (b) ☐ cm   8 cm / 3 cm / 8 cm / 3 cm

   (c) ☐ cm   9 cm / 2 cm / 9 cm / 2 cm

   (d) ☐ cm   7 cm / 5 cm / 7 cm / 5 cm

2. Draw three rectangles with the same perimeter as this square.

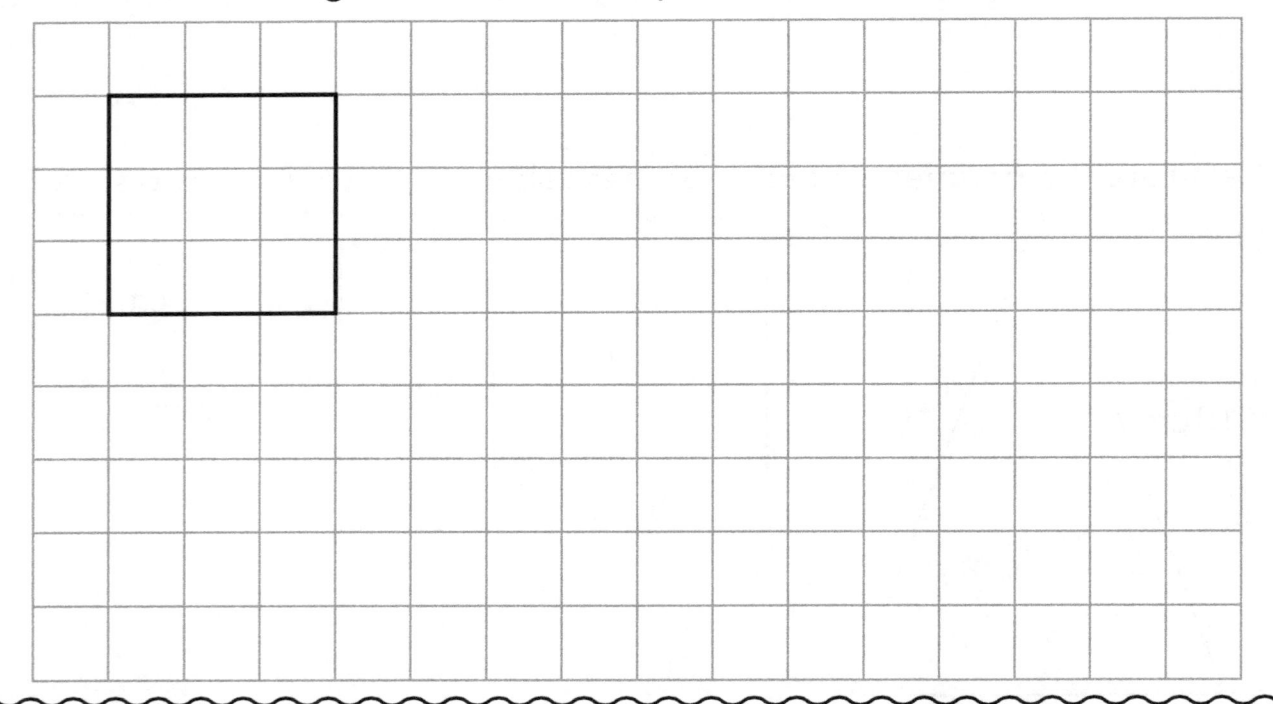

## 👪 Perimeter

Collect boxes of different sizes, items such as tea, shoes or cereal boxes. Draw round the base of each box onto paper or card. Ask your child to place these base templates in order of estimated perimeter length, now measure the perimeters in centimetres and check if the guessed order is correct.

**You will need:** a selection of different shaped boxes, tape measure or ruler.

# Answers

## 1.1 Revision for addition and subtraction of 2-digit numbers
Q1 Check additions total 99
Q2 (a) 54, 73, 51, 76
 (b) 61, 75, 70, 66
 (c) 24, 55, 35, 66
 (d) 36, 82, 29, 75
Q3 Day 1 99, Day 2 99, Day 3 80
 Footballs 84, Basketballs 95, Netballs 99

## 1.2 Addition and subtraction (1)
Q1 (a) 45 (b) 32
 (c) 83 (d) 16
Q2 (a) 85 − 23 = 62
 (b) 46 − 29 = 17
 (c) 52 − 17 = 35

## 1.3 Addition and subtraction (2)
Q1 (a) 15 + 9 = 24
 (b) 33 − 12 = 21
 (c) 48 − 16 = 32
 (d) 35 − 14 = 21
Q2 (a) Tent and sleeping bag
 £63 + £37 = £100
 (b) £19 + £63 = £82
 (c) £50 − £37 = £13

## 1.4 Calculating smartly
Q1 (a) 55
 (b) 79
 (c) 29
 (d) 27
Q2 (a) 85
 (b) 18
 (c) +1, −1, 40 + 42, 82
 (d) +3, +3, 60 − 21, 39
Q3 (a) 60 + 12 = 72
 (b) 67 − 40 = 27
 (c) 30 + 21 = 51
 (d) 90 − 51 = 39 or
 89 − 50 = 39

## 1.5 What number should be in the box?
Q1 (a) 27 + 35 = 62, 35 + 27 = 62,
 62 − 35 = 27, 62 − 27 = 35
 (b) 43 + 28 = 71, 28 + 43 = 71,
 71 − 43 = 28, 71 − 28 = 43

Q2 (a) 55
 (b) 90
 (c) 36
Q3 (a) 28 (b) 16
 (c) 73 (d) 54

## 1.6 Let's revise multiplication
Q1 8, 10, 16, 18, 20, 22, 24
 12, 20, 24, 28, 32, 40, 44
 24, 32, 48, 56, 72, 88, 96
Q2 (a) 12, 24
 (b) 28, 56
 (c) 12, 24
 (d) 48, 96
 (e) 32, 64
 (f) 22, 44
Q3 (a) 3 × 4 = 12
 (b) 2 × 5 = 10
 (c) 5 × 8 = 40

## 1.7 Games of multiplication and division
Q1 (a) 4 days
 (b) 12 days
 (c) 8 days
 (d) 6 days
Q2 (a) 3 × 7 + 6 = 27 or
 4 × 6 + 3 = 27
 4 × 7 − 1 = 27
 (b) 7 × 3 + 6 = 27 or
 6 × 4 + 3 = 27
 7 × 4 − 1 = 27

## 2.1 Multiplying and dividing by 7
Q1 (a) 14 (b) 10 (c) 7
 (d) 3 (e) 42 (f) 11
 (g) 7 (h) 7 (i) 7
 (j) 28 (k) 7 (l) 12
Q2 (a) 21, 49, 28, 63, 42, 84
 (b) 2, 5, 8, 10, 11, 1
Q3 (a) 2 weeks
 (b) 21 balls
 (c) 7 boxes
 (d) 63 drinks
 (e) 9 packs

## 2.2 Multiplying and dividing by 3
Q1 (a) 24 (b) 15 (c) 33
 (d) 27 (e) 21 (f) 10
 (g) 12 (h) 6

 (i) 9 (j) 2
Q2 (a) 4 (b) 2 (c) 2
 (d) 5 (e) 6 (f) 6
Q3 24, 33
 7, 3, 3
 3, 9
Q4 5 trikes

## 2.3 Multiplying and dividing by 6
Q1 As well as being crossed through, the numbers in the 6 times table are circled and yellow
Q2 (a) 6 (b) 30 (c) 54
 (d) 12 (e) 36 (f) 60
 (g) 18 (h) 42 (i) 66
 (j) 24 (k) 48 (l) 72
Q3 (a) = (b) >
 (c) = (d) >

## 2.4 Multiplying and dividing by 9
Q1 (a) 36, 45, 54, 63, 72, 81, 90
 (b) 63, 54, 45, 36, 27, 18, 9
 The digits in each pattern of numbers are reversed
Q2 (a) £5
 (b) 36 pencils
 (c) 8 rows
 (d) 6 groups

## 2.5 Relationships between multiplications of 3, 6 and 9
Q1 Numbers in the 9 times table make diagonal patterns on the number grid. As well as being crossed through, the numbers in the 9 times table are always red and every other one is circled.
Q2 (a) 6 × 3, 6 × 3, 2 × 9, 9 × 2, 3 × 6,
 3 × 6
 (b) 12 × 3, 6 × 6, 4 × 9, 9 × 4,
 6 × 6, 3 × 12
 (c) 18 × 3, 6 × 9, 6 × 9, 9 × 6,
 9 × 6, 3 × 18

## 2.6 Multiplication grid
Play the game

## 2.7 Posing multiplication and division questions (1)

Q1 (a) 6 × 2, 2 × 6, 3 × 4, 4 × 3
 (b) 6 × 3, 3 × 6, 2 × 9, 9 × 2
 (c) 3 × 8, 8 × 3, 6 × 4, 4 × 6
 (d) 4 × 9, 9 × 4, 3 × 12, 12 × 3

Q2 (a) 24 ÷ 6 = 4 hamsters
 (b) 16 ÷ 2 = 8 guinea pigs
 (c) 5 × 2 = 10, 10 × 7 = 70 tins
 (d) 8 × 5 = 40, 40 ÷ 10 = 4 cages
 (e) 12 males, 4 females
    Or 4 males, 12 females
    Or 8 males, 8 females

## 2.8 Posing multiplication and division questions (2)

Q1 (a) 18      (b) 8
 (c) 50      (d) 6

Q2 (a) 28 bricks, 35 bricks
 (b) 32 items
 (c) 50 people
 (d) £6
 (e) 2 flapjacks

## 2.9 Using multiplication and addition to express a number

Q1 (a) 7, 5, 4, 3, 3, 2
 (b) 4, 6, 2, 7, 4, 1

Q2 (a) 28   (b) 31   (c) 35

## 2.10 Division with a remainder

Q1 (a) 5 groups, 1 left over, 16 ÷ 3 = 5 r 1
 (b) 2 groups, 4 left over, 16 ÷ 6 = 2 r 4

Q2 (a) 6 r 2   (b) 8 r 1
 (c) 5 r 3   (d) 7 r 3

Q3 14 sweets

## 2.11 Calculation of division with a remainder (1)

Q1 (a) 2 r 2   (b) 6 r 1
 (c) 4 r 2   (d) 3 r 3

Q2 (a) 9   (b) 5   (c) 5
 (d) 2   (e) 7   (f) 4

Q3 (a) 8 tables, 3 legs left over
 (b) 4 weeks, 2 days

## 2.12 Calculation of division with a remainder (2)

Q1 (a) 14    (b) 33
 (c) 43    (d) 34
 (e) 29    (f) 78

Q2 (a) 9 × 5 + 3 = 48
 (b) 7 × 6 + 3 = 45

Q3 (a) 23 ÷ 5 = 4 r 3, 23 ÷ 4 = 5 r 3
 (b) 20 ÷ 3 = 6 r 2, 20 ÷ 6 = 3 r 2
 (c) 25 ÷ 8 = 3 r 1, 25 ÷ 3 = 8 r 1
 (d) 39 ÷ 4 = 9 r 3, 39 ÷ 9 = 4 r 3

## 2.13 Calculation of division with a remainder (3)

Q1 Greatest number is 23, lowest number is 22

Q2 (a) 13 ÷ 2 = 6 r 1
 (b) 13 ÷ 3 = 4 r 1
 (c) 13 ÷ 4 = 3 r 1

Q3 (a) 3 packs
 (b) 6 packs

## 3.1 Knowing numbers up to 1000 (1)

Q1 (a) 235, two hundred and thirty-five
 (b) 167, one hundred and sixty-seven
 (c) 308, three hundred and eight
 (d) 450, four hundred and fifty

Q2 (a) 3 hundreds + 3 tens + 4 ones
 (b) 5 hundreds + 1 tens + 7 ones
 (c) 4 hundreds + 5 tens + 3 ones
 (d) 6 hundreds + 2 tens + 1 ones

## 3.2 Knowing numbers up to 1000 (2)

Q1 (a) seven hundred and thirty-nine
 (b) 257
 (c) four hundred and fourteen
 (d) 840

Q2 Base ten diagrams drawn correctly
 (a) 280
 (b) 425

Q3 (a) 7̲77
 (b) 8 8̲ 8
 (c) 44 4̲

## 3.3 Number lines (to 1000) (1)

Q1 A  310
 B  400
 C  520
 D  590
 E  650
 F  770

Q2 Check position of arrows

Q3 (a) 239, 240
 (b) 610, 620
 (c) 989, 988
 (d) 500, 550

Q4 742 > 630 > 600 > 471 > 409 > 390 > 389 > 87

## 3.4 Number lines (to 1000) (2)

Q1 Check position of numbers on the number line

Q2 (a) 514, 516, 524
 (b) 340, 360, 365
 (c) 562, 862, 962
 (d) 935, 955, 975

Q3 (a) >   (b) <
 (c) <   (d) >
 (e) =   (f) >
 (g) >   (h) <

Q4 (a) 8   (b) 9   (c) 9
 (d) 6   (e) 2   (f) 7

## 3.5 Fun with the place value chart (1)

Q1 (a) 423   (b) 33
 (c) 604   (d) 13

Q2 Check dots match the number value

Q3 536, 446 or 437

## 3.6 Fun with the place value chart (2)

Q1 Check place value of numbers

Q2 Check place value of numbers

## 4.1 From statistical tables to bar charts

Q1 Robins 6, Finches 8, Sparrows 12, Pigeons 10

Q2 Check graph is accurate

## 4.2 Bar charts (1)
Q1 (a) Check graph is accurate
(b) 13 words
(c) Week 4
(d) Week 1
(e) 5 words

## 4.3 Bar charts (2)
Q1 (a) 7
(b) 8
(c) Sunday
(d) 8
(e) Monday and Wednesday

Q2 (a) Wasps, Ants, Bees, Beetles, Moths
(b) Check bar chart is accurate

## 5.1 Second and minute
Q1 Check times are matched accurately

Q2 (a) hour
(b) weeks
(c) seconds
(d) minutes
(e) days

Q3 (a) 15 minutes
(b) 600 seconds

## 5.2 Times on 12-hour and 24-hour clocks and in Roman numerals
Q1 2:29, 11:15, 6:38, 4:47

Q2 2:15 a.m., 05:32, 11:05 p.m., 20:55
2:20 a.m., 22:20, 11:14 a.m., 12:45

Q3 Seven thirty in the evening
7:30 p.m.    19:30

Twenty past nine in the morning
9:20 a.m.    09:20

Nine fifty-five in the evening
9:55 p.m.    21:55

Quarter past seven at night
7:15 p.m.    19:15

Five past two in the afternoon
2:05 p.m.    14:05

Eleven fifteen in the morning
11:15 a.m.   11:15

## 5.3 Leap years and common years
Q1 (a) 60 minutes
(b) 7 days
(c) 12 months
(d) 365 days
(e) 366 days
(f) Check answer

Q2 (a) 6 months
(b) 3 months
(c) 0 months

## 5.4 Calculating the duration of time
Q1 (a) 20 minutes
(b) 40 minutes
(c) 20 minutes
(d) 35 minutes
(e) 45 minutes

Q2 (a) 6:50 p.m.
(b) 8:25 a.m.
(c) 5 hours 30 minutes
(d) 18:05
(e) 55 minutes

## 6.1 5 threes plus 3 threes equals 8 threes
Q1 (a) $5 \times 3 + 3 \times 3 = 8 \times 3 = 24$
(b) $4 \times 2 + 2 \times 2 = 6 \times 2 = 12$

Q2 (a) $5 \times 5 = 25$
(b) $10 \times 6 = 60$
(c) 24
(d) 45

Q3 (a) £30
(b) 63 books

## 6.2 5 threes minus 3 threes equals 2 threes
Q1 (a) $5 \times 3 - 3 \times 3 = 2 \times 3 = 6$
(b) $4 \times 2 - 3 \times 2 = 1 \times 2 = 2$

Q2 (a) $1 \times 6 = 6$ (b) $4 \times 4 = 16$
(c) $5 \times 5 = 25$ (d) 6
(e) 12 (f) 30

Q3 (a) £14
(b) 8 carrots

## 6.3 Multiplication and division
Q1 (a) 27, 9, 3
(b) 48, 8, 6
(c) 35, 5, 7
(d) 80, 8, 10

Q2 (a) 8 (b) 3 (c) 6
(d) 4 (e) 8 (f) 5

Q3 (a) 36 crayons
(b) 8 boxes, 2 eggs left over
(c) Tom
(d) 7 bunches

## 6.4 Mathematics plaza – dots and patterns
Q1 (a) $3 + 5 = 8$
(b) $6 + 4 = 10$
(c) $4 + 5 = 9$
(d) $7 + 3 = 10$
(e) $4 + 4 = 8$
(f) $6 + 3 = 9$

Q2 (a) 14, 16, 18
(b) 17, 19, 21
(c) 30, 28, 26
(d) 19, 17, 15
(e) 7, 10, 9
(f) 77, 88, 99

Q3 Odd answers: 1 + 2, 2 + 3, 3 + 4, 5 + 6, 4 + 5
Even answers: 6 + 6, 3 + 3, 5 + 5, 4 + 4, 2 + 2

## 6.5 Mathematics plaza – magic square
Q1 (a)

| 4 | 9 | 2 |
|---|---|---|
| 3 | 5 | 7 |
| 8 | 1 | 6 |

(b)

| 6 | 1 | 8 |
|---|---|---|
| 7 | 5 | 3 |
| 2 | 9 | 4 |

Q2 (a)

| 9 | 4 | 11 |
|---|---|----|
| 10 | 8 | 6 |
| 5 | 12 | 7 |

(b)

| 7 | 14 | 9 |
|---|----|---|
| 12 | 10 | 8 |
| 11 | 6 | 13 |

©HarperCollinsPublishers 2018

## 6.6 Numbers to 1000 and beyond

Q1 (a) 3 6 0 8
 (b) 7 9 5 0
 (c) 8 0 0 6
 (d) 4 3 0 5

Q2 (a) Four thousand one hundred and twenty-one, 4121
 (b) Three thousand eight hundred and two, 3802
 (c) Three thousand two hundred and thirty-two, 3232
 (d) Two hundred and thirty, 230

## 6.7 Read, write and compare numbers to 1000 and beyond

Q1 (a) 2511
 (b) 7034
 (c) 9860
 (d) four thousand nine hundred seventy-two
 (e) eight thousand one hundred and three
 (f) six thousand and fifteen

Q2 (a) 1000 + 700 + 20 + 8
 (b) 5000 + 200 + 40 + 0
 (c) 3000 + 500 + 0 + 7
 (d) 9000 + 0 + 10 + 6

Q3 (a) <   (b) >   (c) >
 (d) >   (e) <   (f) >
 (g) <   (h) >   (i) <

## 7.1 Addition and subtraction of whole hundreds and tens (1)

Q1 (a) 7, 70
 (b) 6, 60
 (c) 8, 80
 (d) 4, 40
 (e) 14, 1400
 (f) 2, 200

Q2 (a) 170 T-shirts
 (b) 830 steps
 (c) 170 cm
 (d) 570 visitors

## 7.2 Addition and subtraction of whole hundreds and tens (2)

Q1 (a) 470, 700, 580, 630, 610, 810, 820
 (b) 50, 160, 150, 350, 380, 190, 80

Q2 (a) 810, 10
 (b) 450, 270
 (c) 760, 440
 (d) 750, 290

Q3 (a) 710, 240, 650
 (b) 280, 450, 490

## 7.3 Adding and subtracting 3-digit numbers and ones (1)

Q1 (a) 205   (b) 598
 (c) 403   (d) 496

Q2 (a) 162, 383, 571
 (b) 302, 505, 703
 (c) 226, 447, 658
 (d) 395, 498, 694

Q3 (a) 423, 432, 440, 447
 (b) 262, 259, 266, 257
 (c) 396, 401, 399, 407

## 7.4 Adding and subtracting 3-digit numbers and ones (2)

Q1 (a) 122, 243, 408, 521, 734, 1000
 (b) 110, 231, 396, 509, 722, 988

Q2 (a) 352, 354
    307, 304, 306
    564, 563
 (b) 8
    481, 480, 478
    516, 514
    396, 404, 403

Q3 (a) 191 children
 (b) 135 cm
 (c) 465 passengers
 (d) 253 or 265

## 7.5 Addition with 3-digit numbers (1)

Q1 Check method used for these
 (a) 806   (b) 578
 (c) 708   (d) 652

Q2 Check additions total 999

## 7.6 Addition with 3-digit numbers (2)

Q1 (a) 498   (b) 689   (c) 372
 (d) 691   (e) 836   (f) 706

Q2 (a) 523 children
 (b) 256 pages
 (c) 487 km

Q3  1 7 2
   + 6 5 8
    8 3 0

## 7.7 Subtraction with 3-digit numbers (1)

Q1 Check method used for these
 (a) 151   (b) 336
 (c) 179   (d) 183

Q2 (a) 759 and 426
 (b) 175 and 397
 (c) 397 and 426
 (d) 759 and 175

## 7.8 Subtraction with 3-digit numbers (2)

Q1 (a) 382   (b) 413   (c) 137
 (d) 682   (e) 149   (f) 344

Q2 (a) £164
 (b) £109
 (c) £48
 (d) £61
 (e) £92
 (f) £181

## 7.9 Estimating addition and subtraction with 3-digit numbers (1)

Q1 380 450 510 340 740 700
   400 400 500 300 700 700

Q2 (a) 661, 660
 (b) 885, 890
 (c) 759, 760

Q3 (a) 792, 800
 (b) 915, 900
 (c) 588, 600

Q4 (a) 886, 885, 884
 (b) 160, 161, 162
 (c) 730, 729, 728

## 7.10 Estimating addition and subtraction with 3-digit numbers (2)

Q1 (a) 562, 563, 564, 565
 (b) 453, 452, 451, 450

Q2 (a) 14 m
 (b) 57 m
 (c) 235 m
 (d) 77 m

## 8.1 Unit fractions and tenths

Q1 (a) 2 stars
 (b) 4 balls
 (c) 4 flags

Q2  (a) 4 blue balloons
    (b) 2 green balloons
    (c) 3 yellow balloons
    (d) 6 red balloons
    (e) 8 orange balloons
        1 balloon is left white
Q3  (a) $\frac{4}{10}, \frac{5}{10}, \frac{7}{10}$
    (b) $\frac{3}{10}, \frac{6}{10}, \frac{9}{10}$

## 8.2 Non-unit fractions
Q1  (a) $\frac{1}{6}$
    (b) $\frac{1}{5}$
    (c) $\frac{3}{6}$ or $\frac{1}{2}$
    (d) $\frac{2}{4}$ or $\frac{1}{2}$
    (e) $\frac{1}{7}$
    (f) $\frac{4}{8}$ or $\frac{1}{2}$
Q2  Check fractions coloured in flag design
Q3  (a) $\frac{1}{8}, \frac{2}{8}, \frac{3}{8}, \frac{6}{8}, \frac{7}{8}$
    (b) $\frac{2}{10}, \frac{3}{10}, \frac{4}{10}, \frac{7}{10}, \frac{8}{10}$

## 8.3 Equivalent fractions
Q1  (a) $\frac{2}{4} = \frac{1}{2}$
    (b) $\frac{2}{8} = \frac{1}{4}$
    (c) $\frac{3}{9} = \frac{1}{3}$
    (d) $\frac{2}{10} = \frac{1}{5}$
Q2  (a) $\frac{5}{10} = \frac{1}{2}$
    (b) $\frac{1}{3} = \frac{2}{6}$
    (c) $\frac{4}{16} = \frac{1}{4}$
    (d) $\frac{1}{2} = \frac{3}{6}$
Q3  (a) $\frac{3}{4}$
    (b) $\frac{2}{12}$
    (c) $\frac{3}{30}$

## 8.4 Addition and subtraction of simple fractions
Q1  (a) $\frac{5}{7}$
    (b) $\frac{8}{9}$
    (c) $\frac{7}{8}$
    (d) $\frac{8}{10}$
    (e) $\frac{6}{7}$

Q2  (a) $\frac{3}{10}$
    (b) $\frac{2}{9}$
    (c) $\frac{1}{5}$
    (d) $\frac{4}{7}$
    (e) $\frac{4}{9}$

## 9.1 Multiplying by whole tens and hundreds (1)
Q1  (a) 18, 180, 1800
    (b) 28, 280, 2800
    (c) 48, 480, 4800
Q2  (a) <         (b) =
    (c) =         (d) >
    (e) >         (f) >
Q3  (a) 300       (b) 2
    (c) 400       (d) 7
Q4  80 × 3 and 40 × 6
    10 × 8 and 40 × 2
    60 × 8 and 80 × 6
    50 × 3 and 30 × 5
    60 × 6 and 90 × 4
    60 × 3 and 30 × 6

## 9.2 Multiplying by whole tens and hundreds (2)
Q1  (a) 35, 350, 350, 3500
    (b) 24, 240, 240, 2400
    (c) 36, 3600, 3600, 3600
Q2  (a) 180
    (b) 2400
    (c) 7 × 30 = 210
    (d) 8 × 400 = 3200
Q3  (a) 180 pencils
    (b) 1200 km

## 9.3 Writing number sentences
Q1  (a) 6 × 11 × 3 = 198, £198
    (b) 2 × 12 × 4 = 96, £96
    (c) 4 × 20 × 3 = 240, 240 passengers
Q2  (a) 4 × 35, £140
    (b) 7 × 12, 84 kg
    (c) 50 ÷ 25 = 2, 60 kg

## 9.4 Multiplying a 2-digit number by a 1-digit number (1)
Q1  (a) 150, 5, 150 + 5 = 155
    (b) 160, 36, 160 + 36 = 196
    (c) 160, 48, 160 + 48 = 208
    (d) 60, 42, 60 + 42 = 102
Q2  (a) 172       (b) 141
    (c) 171       (d) 184
Q3  (a) 95 km
    (b) 168 hours
    (c) £1.77

## 9.5 Multiplying a 2-digit number by a 1-digit number (2)
Q1  222, drinks cost £2.22
    Check the answer: 222, 210, 12, 210 + 12 = 222
Q2  (a) 288       (b) 105
    (c) 140       (d) 258
Q3  (a) 54 × 6 = 324
    (b) 56 × 4 = 224
    (c) 64 × 5 = 320

## 9.6 Multiplying a 2-digit number by a 1-digit number (3)
A 168, N 186, Z 158, H 153,
A 168, M 120, T 144, A 168,
I 194, A 168, G 184, T 144,
S 171, M 120
AMAZING AT MATHS

## 9.7 Multiplying a 3-digit number by a 1-digit number (1)
Q1  (a) 2000, 100, 5, 2000 + 100 + 5
    (b) 600, 80, 12, 600 + 80 + 12
    (c) 1500, 90, 24, 1500 + 90 + 24
    (d) 800, 280, 20, 800 + 280 + 20
Q2  (a) 2478      (b) 1164
    (c) 5436      (d) 2910
Q3  (a) 768 people
    (b) 960 teabags
    (c) 900 cm

## 9.8 Multiplying a 3-digit number by a 1-digit number (2)
Q1  (a) 400, 448      (b) 450, 459
    (c) 2400, 2524    (d) 1600, 1560
Q2  (a) 2250 g        (b) 1520 g
    (c) 1180 g        (d) 980 g

## 9.9 Practice and exercise
**Q1** (a) <  (b) >  (c) <
   (d) >  (e) =  (f) <
**Q2** (a) 1520
   (b) 3240
   (c) 1180
   (d) 2448
**Q3** (a) the same as
   (b) more than
   (c) less than
   (d) the same as

## 9.10 Dividing whole tens and whole hundreds
**Q1** (a) 8  (b) 9  (c) 7
**Q2** (a) 70, 7  (b) 60, 6  (c) 30, 3
   (d) 90, 9  (e) 90, 9  (f) 50, 5
**Q3** (a) 7 tiles
   (b) 90 pages
   (c) 5 laps

## 9.11 Dividing a 2-digit number by a 1-digit number (1)
**Q1** (a) 9 × 4 = 36, 36 ÷ 9 = 4,
   4 × 9 = 36, 36 ÷ 4 = 9
   (b) 5 × 9 = 45, 45 ÷ 9 = 5,
   9 × 5 = 45, 45 ÷ 5 = 9
   (c) 6 × 7 = 42, 42 ÷ 6 = 7,
   7 × 6 = 42, 42 ÷ 7 = 6
   (d) 7 × 8 = 56, 56 ÷ 7 = 8,
   8 × 7 = 56, 56 ÷ 8 = 7
**Q2** (a) 7  (b) 5  (c) 9
   (d) 7  (e) 7  (f) 9
**Q3** (a) 6, 7, 13
   (b) 4, 10, 14
   (c) 4, 10, 14

## 9.12 Dividing a 2-digit number by a 1-digit number (2)
**Q1** (a) 16  (b) 15  (c) 17  (d) 11
**Q2** (a) 29  (b) 17  (c) 17
**Q3** (a) 28 children
   (b) 15 packs
   (c) 14 weeks

## 9.13 Dividing a 2-digit number by a 1-digit number (3)
**Q1** (a) 16 r 1
   (b) 19 r 3
   (c) 13 r 3
   (d) 28 r 2
**Q2** (a) 23 r 1
   (b) 18 r 3
   (c) 20 r 1
**Q3** (a) 21 full rows with 2 children in the last row
   (b) 5 teachers

## 9.14 Dividing a 2-digit number by a 1-digit number (4)
**Q1** (a) 18, 9
   (b) 28, 14
   (c) 34, 17
   (d) 24, 12
**Q2** (a) 12, 8, 6  (b) 20, 15, 12
   (c) 12, 6, 4  (d) 18, 12, 9
**Q3** 46 lettuces

## 9.15 Dividing a 2-digit number by a 1-digit number (5)
**Q1** (a) 18 r 3
   (b) 12 r 3
   (c) 9 r 3
**Q2** r 1 → 19 ÷ 3, 82 ÷ 9
   r 2 → 74 ÷ 8, 23 ÷ 7
   r 3 → 38 ÷ 5, 27 ÷ 4
   r 4 → 40 ÷ 6, 44 ÷ 8
**Q3** (a) 232 beads
   (b) 19 necklaces
   (c) 4 blue beads

## 9.16 Dividing a 3-digit number by a 1-digit number (1)
**Q1** (a) 121 r 1
   (b) 243
   (c) 153 r 3
**Q2** (a) 121 r 1
   (b) 243
   (c) 126 r 2
**Q3** (a) 736, 924, 496, 612, 548
   (b) 496, 736

## 9.17 Dividing a 3-digit number by a 1-digit number (2)
**Q1** (a) 186, 181
   (b) 186
   (c) 195
   (d) 181
**Q2** 107, 119, 131
   The next two numbers after 140 are 143 and 155

## 9.18 Dividing a 3-digit number by a 1-digit number (3)
**Q1** (a) 111 r 3  (b) 206 r 1
   (c) 167 r 2  (d) 87 r 7
**Q2** (a) 137  (b) 43
   (c) 75  (d) 123
**Q3** 240, 180, 144, 120, 90, 80
   168, 112, 84, 56, 48, 42

## 9.19 Application of division
**Q1** (a) 52 weeks, 1 day left over
   (b) 62 tiles
   (c) 84 cars
   (d) 71 lengths, 3 m left over
**Q2** 147 badges

## 9.20 Finding the total price
**Q1** Bicycle tyre total price: £70
   Car number of wheels: 4
   Lorry tyre, price per wheel: £70
**Q2** (a) ×
   (b) ÷
   (c) ÷
**Q3** (a) 14 egg cartons
   (b) £72
   (c) £285
   (d) 595 adults and children

## 10.1 Angles
**Q1** (a) 3 angles, 4 angles, 4 angles, 4, angles, 5 angles, 4 angles
   (b) Check dots are drawn on right angles
**Q2** Check angles are accurate

©HarperCollins*Publishers* 2018

## 10.2 Identifying different types of line (1)

Q1 Check the three horizontal lines are ticked

Q2 Check seven vertical posts are coloured red

Q3 (a) Three-quarter turn
(b) Quarter turn
(c) Complete turn
(d) Half turn

Q4 (a) true
(b) false
(c) true
(d) true

## 10.3 Identifying different types of line (2)

Q1 a and d are vertical

Q2 Check pairs of parallel lines are identified

Q3 Check 3 lines are horizontal and parallel to each other

Q4 E

## 10.4 Drawing 2-D shapes and making 3-D shapes

Q1 Check shapes are drawn accurately

Q2 Check cuboid is drawn accurately

## 10.5 Length: metre, centimetre and millimetre

Q1 (a) 7 cm
(b) 10 cm
(c) 6 cm

Q2 (a) >        (b) >
(c) =        (d) <
(e) =        (f) <

Q3 (a) cm
(b) cm
(c) m
(d) m

## 10.6 Perimeters of simple 2-D shapes (1)

Q1 (a) 14 cm  (b) 14 cm  (c) 12 cm

Q2 Check shape has a perimeter of 16 cm

Q3 (a) 27 cm  (b) 20 cm  (c) 22 cm

## 10.7 Perimeters of simple 2-D shapes (2)

Q1 (a) 16 cm        (b) 22 cm
(c) 22 cm        (d) 24 cm

Q2 Check rectangles have a perimeter of 12 cm

# Notes

# Notes

# Collins

William Collins' dream of knowledge for all began with the publication of his first book in 1819.

A self-educated mill worker, he not only enriched millions of lives, but also founded a flourishing publishing house. Today, staying true to this spirit, Collins books are packed with inspiration, innovation and practical expertise. They place you at the centre of a world of possibility and give you exactly what you need to explore it.

Collins. Freedom to teach.

Published by Collins
An imprint of HarperCollins*Publishers*
The News Building
1 London Bridge Street
London
SE1 9GF

Browse the complete Collins catalogue at
www.collins.co.uk

© HarperCollins*Publishers* Limited 2018

10 9 8 7 6 5 4 3 2 1

978-0-00-824147-6

Author: Paul Broadbent

Homework Guide Series Editor: Amanda Simpson

Practice Books Series Editor: Professor Lianghuo Fan

All rights reserved. No part of this publication may be reproduced, stored in a retrieval system, or transmitted in any form by any means, electronic, mechanical, photocopying, recording or otherwise, without the prior written permission of the Publisher or a licence permitting restricted copying in the United Kingdom issued by the Copyright Licensing Agency Ltd., Barnard's Inn, 86 Fetter Lane, London, EC4A 1EN.

British Library Cataloguing in Publication Data

A catalogue record for this publication is available from the British Library.

Publishing Managers: Fiona McGlade and Lizzie Catford
In-house Senior Editor: Mike Appleton
In-house Editorial Assistant: August Stevens
Project Manager: Emily Hooton
Copy Editor: Karen Williams
Proofreader: Jo Kemp
Answers: James Quarrington and Paul Wrangles
Cover design: Kevin Robbins and East China Normal University Press Ltd.
Internal design: 2Hoots Publishing Services Ltd
Typesetting: 2Hoots Publishing Services Ltd
Illustrations: QBS
Production: Sarah Burke

Printed and bound by CPI Group (UK) Ltd, Croydon, CR0 4YY

MIX
Paper from responsible sources
FSC C007454

This book is produced from independently certified FSC paper to ensure responsible forest management.

For more information visit:
www.harpercollins.co.uk/green